CAMBRIDGE ENGLISH
Worldwide
Student's Book Four

ANDREW LITTLEJOHN & DIANA HICKS

PUBLISHED BY THE PRESS SYNDICATE OF THE UNIVERSITY OF CAMBRIDGE
The Pitt Building, Trumpington Street, Cambridge, United Kingdom

CAMBRIDGE UNIVERSITY PRESS
The Edinburgh Building, Cambridge CB2 2RU, UK
40 West 20th Street, New York, NY 10011-4211, USA
10 Stamford Road, Oakleigh, VIC 3166, Australia
Ruiz de Alarcón 13, 28014 Madrid, Spain
Dock House, The Waterfront, Cape Town 8001, South Africa

http://www.cambridge.org

© Cambridge University Press 2000

This book is in copyright. Subject to statutory exception
and to the provisions of relevant collective licensing agreements,
no reproduction of any part may take place without
the written permission of Cambridge University Press.

First published 2000
Reprinted 2001

Printed in the United Kingdom at the University Press, Cambridge.

ISBN 0 521 78376 3 Student's Book
ISBN 0 521 78377 1 Workbook
ISBN 0 521 78379 8 Listening and Speaking Pack
ISBN 0 521 78378 X Teacher's Book
ISBN 0 521 78380 1 Class Cassette
ISBN 0 521 776686 A to Z of Methodology

Contents

Map of *Cambridge English Worldwide 4* 4

THEME

A A world of knowledge
Around the book 6
1 A new beginning 8
2 TEST YOUR ENGLISH Looking back 10
3 REVISION 12
   EVALUATION Vocabulary 16

B Visions of the future
Around the Theme 17
4 TOPIC AND LANGUAGE Our future 18
5 TOPIC AND LANGUAGE After school 22
6 OUT AND ABOUT WITH ENGLISH What should you do? 26
   EVALUATION Writing 28

C Media stories
Around the Theme 29
7 TOPIC AND LANGUAGE The magic box 30
8 TOPIC AND LANGUAGE The news 34
9 ALL ABOUT... The news 38
   EVALUATION Listening 40

D Spinning in space
Around the Theme 41
10 TOPIC AND LANGUAGE Messages through space 42
11 OUT AND ABOUT WITH ENGLISH Too afraid to speak 46
12 REVISION 48
    EVALUATION Reading 52

E Wonders of the world
Around the Theme 53
13 TOPIC AND LANGUAGE Our heritage 54
14 TOPIC AND LANGUAGE Natural Wonders 58
15 ALL ABOUT... Mysteries of the past 62
    EVALUATION Speaking 64

F The time of our life
Around the Theme 65
16 TOPIC AND LANGUAGE Free time 66
17 OUT AND ABOUT WITH ENGLISH The volleyball team 70
18 REVISION 72
    EVALUATION Grammar 76

Optional units
A OUT AND ABOUT WITH ENGLISH A friend in need 78
B FLUENCY Write a story 80
C CULTURE MATTERS The USA – a melting pot 81
D FLUENCY A letter for the world 83
E OUT AND ABOUT WITH ENGLISH A sponsored fast 84
F CULTURE MATTERS Discover Canada! 86

A heritage map of the world 88
Irregular verbs 90
Help yourself list 91
Wordlist/Index 93
Thanks and acknowledgments 96

Map of *Cambridge English Worldwide 4*

THEME	UNIT		UNIT	
A A world of knowledge **Curriculum links:** *Learning to learn* – language record. *History* – Loch Ness surveys, exporting ice; *Environmental Studies* – transport; *Geography* – around the world. *Learning to learn* – vocabulary	**1**	**A new beginning** 8 Learning about people in your class; getting ready to learn English.	**2**	**TEST YOUR ENGLISH** 10 **Looking back** A test covering: Past simple, Past perfect, 'used to', relative clauses, Past continuous, Present perfect, Future simple.
B Visions of the future **Curriculum links:** *Environmental and Social Studies* – our future society; *Personal and Social Education* – the right job, the future of work; *Moral Education* – obligations and friendship; *Learning to learn* – writing.	**4**	**TOPIC AND LANGUAGE** 18 **Our future** Images of the future; futurologists' predictions; a letter to world leaders. *Language:* 'will', 'going to', Future perfect. *Vocabulary areas:* social change, technology. *Revision:* preposition of time	**5**	**TOPIC AND LANGUAGE** 22 **After school** Your personal future; the right job for you; jobs in the future. *Language:* phrasal verbs. *Vocabulary areas:* work and jobs.
C Media stories **Curriculum links:** *Social Studies* – effects of television; *Media and Communication Studies* – the news; *Learning to learn* – listening	**7**	**TOPIC AND LANGUAGE** 30 **The magic box** Programmes on television; the effects of television. *Language:* Past simple and Present perfect. *Vocabulary areas:* television and social effects.	**8**	**TOPIC AND LANGUAGE** 34 **The news** The news; selecting stories. *Language:* question tags; discussing ideas. *Vocabulary:* negative and positive words; types of news stories; describing the news.
D Spinning in space **Curriculum links:** *Science* – how signals are transmitted; *Learning to learn* – reading	**10**	**TOPIC AND LANGUAGE** 42 **Messages through space** Television and satellites. *Language:* Present passive. *Vocabulary:* talking about broadcasting.	**11**	**OUT AND ABOUT WITH ENGLISH** 46 **Too afraid to speak** 'Telling tales'; reporting bad behaviour; personal safety. *Language:* question tags, idioms.
E Wonders of the world **Curriculum links:** *History* – famous natural and man-made sites; *Cultural Studies* – history of Canada; *Social Education* – supporting charities; *Learning to learn* – speaking	**13**	**TOPIC AND LANGUAGE** 54 **Our heritage** Preserving famous places; mysteries from the past. *Language:* second conditional; speculating. *Vocabulary:* looking after things.	**14**	**TOPIC AND LANGUAGE** 58 **Natural wonders** Some natural wonders of the world; protecting those places. *Language:* Past passive. *Vocabulary:* natural features.
F The time of our life *Sport* – the value of sport; *Moral Education* – rules; *Learning to learn* – grammar.	**16**	**TOPIC AND LANGUAGE** 66 **Free time** Leisure, sport; learning from each other. *Language:* the passive. *Vocabulary areas:* leisure activities, sports, politics.	**17**	**OUT AND ABOUT WITH ENGLISH** 70 **The volleyball team** The importance of rules; should rules always be followed? *Language:* idioms; Present continuous for future reference, idioms.

UNIT			OPTIONAL UNITS		
3	**REVISION** Practice of: Past continuous, Present perfect, Future simple, First conditional, Past perfect, 'used to'. *Evaluation*: How do you learn vocabulary?	12	A	**OUT AND ABOUT WITH ENGLISH** **A friend in need** Friendship and loyalty; Is it ever right to lie? *Language*: Present perfect; Future simple; offers with 'will'; describing objects and past actions, idioms.	78
6	**OUT AND ABOUT WITH ENGLISH** **What should you do?** Helping someone against their will; obligations and friendship. *Language*: conditionals, idioms. *Evaluation*: How do you practise writing in English?	26	B	**FLUENCY** **Write a story** Creative writing.	80
9	**ALL ABOUT...** **The news** News stories from around the world. *Fluency practice*: reading and writing. *Evaluation*: How do you practise listening in English?	38	C	**CULTURE MATTERS** **USA – a melting pot** The peoples of the USA; slavery and the history of black Americans; emigration and immigration in your country.	81
12	**REVISION** Revision of Themes B, C and D. *Language*: Future simple, 'going to', Present perfect, Question tags. *Evaluation*: How do you practise reading in English?	48	D	**FLUENCY** **A letter for the world** A letter to world leaders.	83
15	**ALL ABOUT...** **The mysteries of the past** The mysteries of sites in Africa, North America and South America. *Fluency practice*: reading and writing. *Evaluation*: How do you practise speaking in English?	62	E	**OUT AND ABOUT WITH ENGLISH** **A sponsored fast** Giving money to charities. *Language*: Past passive; second conditional; challenging and criticising ideas, idioms.	84
18	**REVISION** **Revision of Themes E and F** *Language*: 'unless', second conditional, Past passive. *Evaluation*: How do you learn grammar in English?	72	F	**CULTURE MATTERS** **Discover Canada!** Famous places in Canada; Native Canadians and settlers in Canada; Canada and your country.	86

Theme A
A world of knowledge

1 What's in your book?

1.1 Looking through the book

Look through your book. What are the units about?
If you want to find a particular word, a grammar area, a unit or the details of a theme, where can you look?

1.2 Four places

Where do these extracts come from? Match each extract to the correct section. What is each section for?

Contents   Map of the book   a Theme page   Wordlist/index

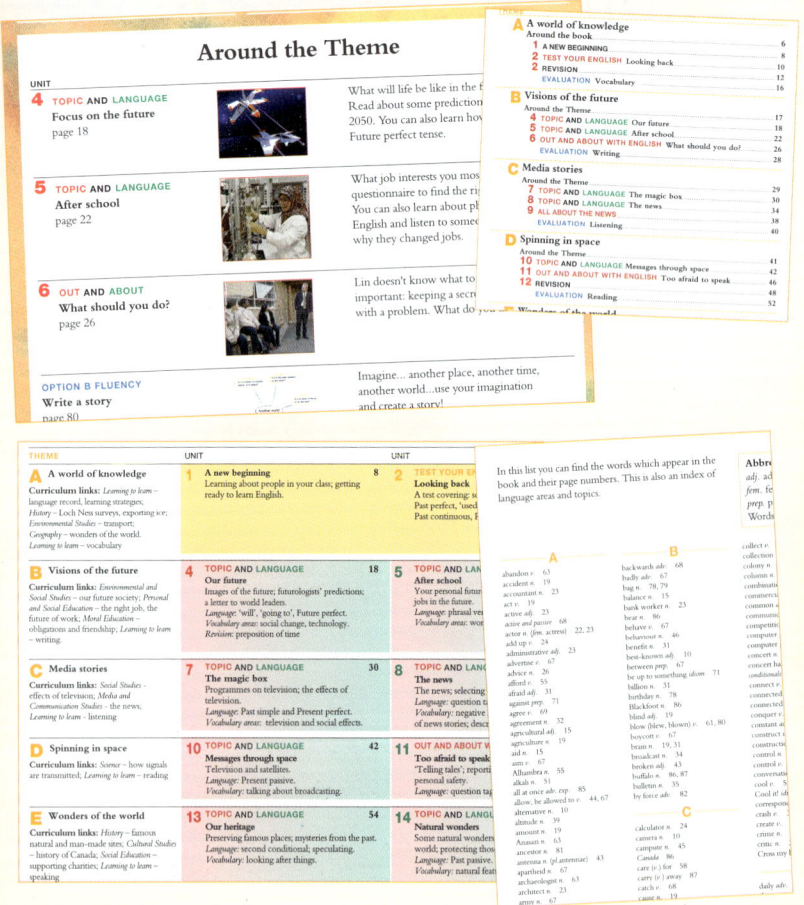

2 Take a look at your book

2.1 Some questions

Look through your book.
Can you answer these questions?

How many units are in each theme?
What are the Out and About Units about?
Where can you find Revision exercises?
How many Optional Units are there?

2.2 Around the book

Look at the pictures. Can you find the picture in each Theme?
Read about the Themes. In which Theme can you:

– find out about messages in space?
– find out about World Heritage sites?
– learn about the effects of television?
– learn about some predictions for the future?
– talk about your views on breaking the rules?

Around the book

THEME

A
A world of knowledge

Are there any new things in your life? In Unit 1 you can find out more about your classmates' lives. In Unit 2 you can test yourself in English and get some more practice in Unit 3.

B
Visions of the future

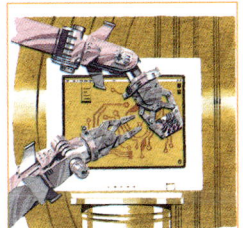

Will life in the future be better or worse? Learn about some predictions in Unit 4. Find out which is the best job for you in Unit 5. In Unit 6, Lin doesn't know what to do. Should she keep a secret or try to help her friend? What do you think?

C
Media stories

Television is wonderful but it can also be bad. In Unit 7 read about how it can affect us and our lives. What kinds of stories do we see in the newspapers and on the television news? Find out in Unit 8. Read some more newspaper stories in Unit 9.

D
Spinning in space

How do messages travel around the world? Unit 10 describes how important satellites are for modern communications. In Unit 11 Samantha hears something on the TV news which makes her worried. Who should she tell? Do some revision in Unit 12.

E
Wonders of the world

Why are some places in the world protected by an International organisation? Find out in Unit 13. Why do we need to protect our natural environment? Learn some of the reasons in Unit 14. What kinds of mysteries surround some of the world's most famous places? Find out in Unit 15.

F
The time of our life

How do you spend your free time? Do you have any hobbies? In Unit 16 you can read about the different ways in which sport is important. In Unit 17 Tom's got a problem with the Volleyball team. Do you think it's all right for the volleyball team to break the rules?

Finding out about people in your class; your language record

1 *Learning about each other*

2 *Language Record*

1 A new beginning

1 Finding out

1.1 Personal information

Here is some information about a person. What can you guess about that person? For example:

Her favourite TV programme is called 'In the Street'.

swimming	blue	disco music
14	Computer Studies	pasta
computer programmer	cats	'In the Street'

1.2 All about you

Think about yourself and write down some information.

- New things in my life:
- Things I hate:
- Things I love:
- Things I have just done:
- Places I want to go:
- Places I've been:
- Things I am good at:
- My favourite things:
- A hobby or special interest:

Now copy this diagram and write in nine pieces of information.

1.3 Play a game

Work with a partner. Draw another diagram, and then take it in turns to put information in the squares. Tell your partner about the information when you write it on the diagram. The first person to make a straight line is the winner!

Play two or three games – use different information each time.

1.4 Learn about your class

You can make a poster with information about each person in the class. Put all your diagrams from Exercise 1.3 on a large sheet of paper with your names. If you want to know more about a piece of information, talk to the person concerned.

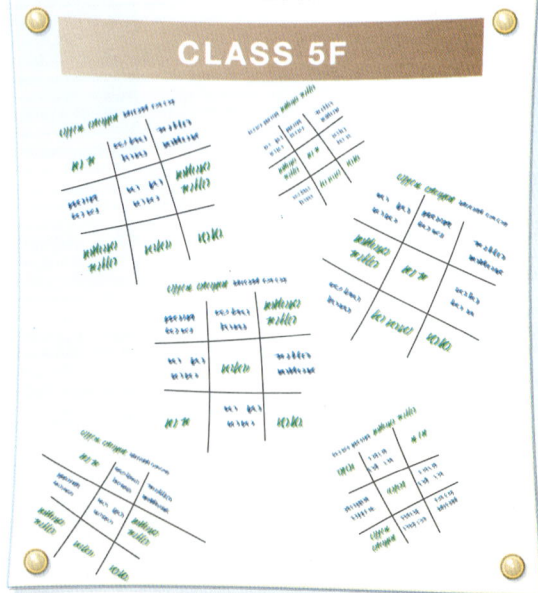

8   Unit 1   A new beginning

2 Your Language Record

2.1 Look at the Units

Do you have a *Language Record* that you used with Book 3? You can start a new one for Book 4. A *Language Record* will help you learn more quickly.

Look at Theme B, Units 4 and 5. Can you find an exercise that asks you to work with your *Language Record*? What does it ask you to do?

Look at the other Themes. Where do the *Language Record* exercises always appear? What do they always ask you to do?

2.2 Prepare your Language Record

Your *Language Record* needs to have three parts.

Record of Language Use
Here you can keep a record of all the words, idioms and phrases you learn.

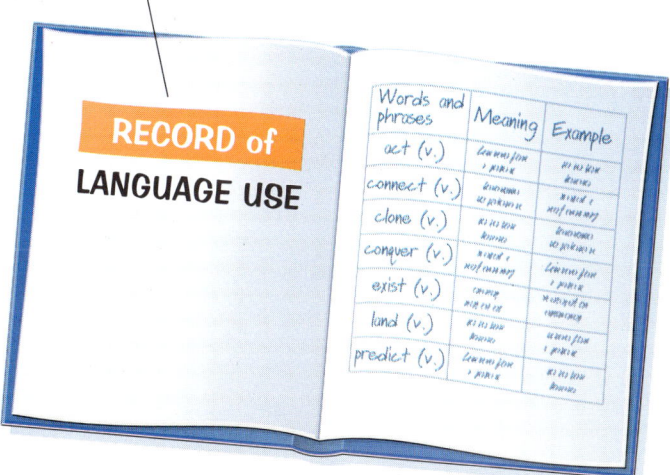

Word Groups
Here you can put words into groups.

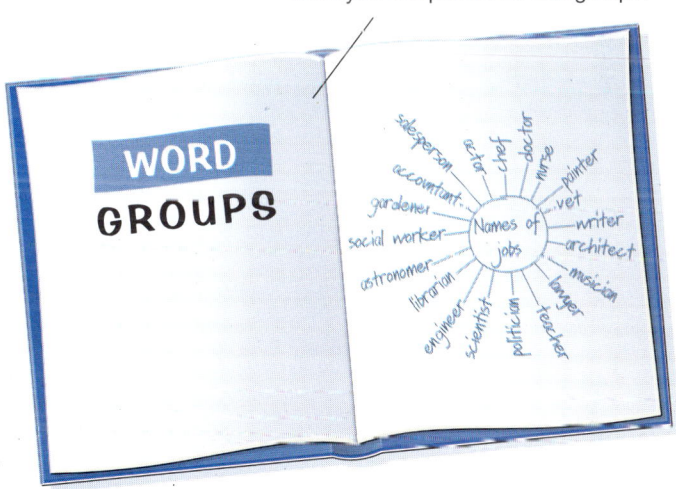

Grammar Record
Here you can make notes about grammar points and example sentences.

2.3 Where does it go?

Where in your *Language Record* would you put these things?

- the names of hobbies
- notes about the Future perfect
- some ways to disagree with someone
- different words to describe nature
- notes about the Past perfect
- words from Unit 8
- idioms from Unit 6

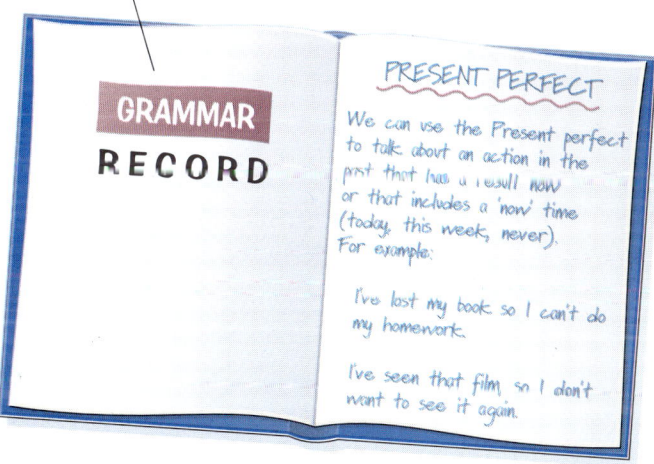

Use your *Language Record* now! Note down any interesting words and phrases from Unit 1.

Unit 1 A new beginning 9

A test covering language from Student's Book 3.

1 *Past simple, Past continuous*
WB Ex. 1

2 *Present perfect*

3 *Future simple*

4 *Past perfect*

5 *'used to', relative clauses*

2 Looking back
Test your English

A world of mystery

1 **Is there a monster in Loch Ness?**

Read about the Loch Ness monster. Circle the correct answer.

1   **a** were driving   **b** drive   **c** are driving
2   **a** was using   **b** used   **c** uses
3   **a** was swimming   **b** swims   **c** is swimming

The 'monster' in Loch Ness, Scotland, is one of the world's best-known mysteries.

In 1933, a man and a woman said that they saw 'an enormous animal' in the water while they [1]..................... beside the lake. Since then many people have seen the monster and some people have taken photographs.

In 1972 and 1975, an American scientific expedition [2]..................... special cameras to search for the monster. They took photographs of a large animal while it [3]..................... under water, but many people said the photographs were not clear enough. In 1987, a British expedition searched the lake with sonar equipment but they found nothing.

Alternatives for the future

2 **Transport problems**

Read about attempts to reduce problems with car traffic. Circle the correct answer.

Many governments have tried different solutions to the problem of car traffic.

1 Some cities, for example Mexico City, ... controls on the use of cars. Cars can only come into the city centre on certain days in the week.
  a have introduced   **b** introduce
  c were introducing

2 Some cities .... to improve public transport systems. Light railway systems and underground trains now cross many cities quickly.
  a have tried   **b** try   **c** were trying

3 A new development is Magnetic Levitation trains which travel at high speed without polluting the atmosphere. In Germany, they .... construction of a Maglev train from Berlin to Hamburg.
  a have begun   **b** begin   **c** were beginning

10   Unit 2   Looking back

3 Your predictions

One hundred years from now, how will we live?
Choose three questions and write a sentence to answer each one.

- What will we eat?
- How will we travel?
- How will we communicate?
- Where will we go in space?
- What will our houses look like?

The world of music

4 Before the concert began

Look at this picture of a pop concert. What had these people done before the concert began? Write three sentences.

1 The engineers – test all the equipment.
   The engineers had tested all the equipment.
2 The cleaners – clean the concert hall
3 The ticket office – sell all the tickets
4 The musicians – practise their songs

Changing views

5 Ice in summer

5.1 In Norway

Ice in summer is a very recent thing. What did they do hundreds of years ago? Read the text and circle the answers.

1 Hundreds of years ago, people .... electricity but they had ice in their drinks in the summer.
   a didn't use to have   b weren't using
   c aren't using

2 How .... ?
   a did they use to get it?   b do they use it?
   c do they get it?

3 Workers used to sail in ships from England to Norway. There, they .... large blocks of ice from the lakes. They then took them back to England on the ships.
   a used to cut   b were using   c were cutting

Inside an icehouse

5.2 In England

Read what happened to the ice in England. Circle the correct answers.

1 Rich people, ... lived in large houses, often had a separate 'icehouse' where they put the ice.
   a who   b which

2 The icehouse, ... was usually underground, was very cold. This meant that the ice melted very slowly.
   a who   b which

3 Ice was very expensive but it was very popular with rich people, ... used to put it in their drinks when it was hot.

Unit 2 Test your English 11

Revision exercises

1 *Past continuous*

2 *Present perfect*

WB Ex. 1

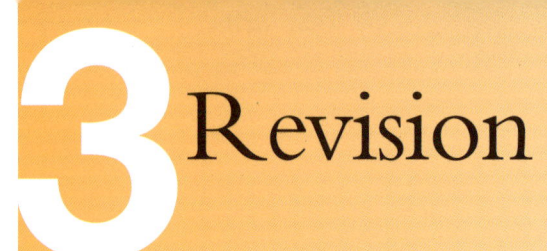

3 Revision

1 What were they doing?

In AD 79 the volcano Vesuvius in southern Italy erupted very suddenly and destroyed the cities of Pompeii and Herculaneum. The bodies of 2000 people have been found in Pompeii. Most of the people died immediately.

What were they doing when the volcano erupted? Look at the picture and write sentences about the people. For example:

Some people were eating dinner.

2 What's the result?

2.1 Make some sentences

Put the verb in the Present perfect. Then match the two parts of the sentence.

1. We *have cooked* the dinner (cook) …
2. We ……………… our exams (finish) …
3. I ……………… the letter (write) …
4. He ……………… there for 10 years (live) …
5. The film ……………… (finish) …
6. She ……………… her glasses (lose) …

a … so he knows everyone in the street.
b … so now we have to go home.
c … so she can't read the paper.
d … so now we can eat.
e … so now I need a stamp.
f … so now we can go on holiday.

2.2 Around the world

Paula Edmonds is sailing around the world alone.
She is talking on her radio telephone to the control station.
Complete the conversation.

CONTROL STATION: Good morning, Paula. How are you?
PAULA: Fine now, thanks.
CONTROL STATION: *Has* the storm *stopped* now? (stop)
PAULA: Yes, It has. It was terrible last night.
CONTROL STATION: Has it ¹……………… any damage to the yacht? (do)
PAULA: Yes, a bit. I ²……………… the sails already and now I'm going to check inside. (check)
CONTROL STATION: ³……………… you ……………… anything? (lose)
PAULA: Yes, I think I ⁴……………… some maps. They're covered in water. (lose)
CONTROL STATION: So you ⁵……………… not ……………… your position yet today? (check)
PAULA: No, not yet. I've been too busy repairing everything.
CONTROL STATION: ⁶……………… any of the other boats ……………… in touch with you yet? (be)
PAULA: No, they haven't. I'm really worried about that.
CONTROL STATION: OK. No problem. I'll call you back in half an hour.
PAULA: OK, thanks. Over and out.

Unit 3   Revision   13

3 Future simple, first conditional
WB Ex. 2

4 Past perfect
WB Ex. 3

5 'used to'
WB Ex. 4

6 relative clauses

3 How can I help?

3.1 Moving house

Mrs Martin and her son Jack are moving to another flat. She has written a list of things she must do. Jack's friends want to help. What do they say?

Moving: jobs to do
1. Find boxes
2. Clean the flat
3. Pack clothes
4. Throw things away
5. Take down curtains
6. Organise books and CDs

3.2 If you …

At different ages adults give children different advice. Look at the pictures. What do you think the adults are saying to the children?

1 year   2 years   4 years   6 years   8 years   10 years   12 years

1 If you go up the stairs, *you will fall*
2 If you touch the fire, …
3 If you don't hold my hand, …
4 If you climb that tree, …
5 If you eat …
6 If you wear those shoes, …
7 If you don't go to bed soon, …

Write two more sentences. What do adults advise you to do?

8 If you …
9 If you …

4 What happened before?

Look carefully at the picture. Rosa and Roderick have got married. Can you find seven things that had happened just before this picture was taken? Write a sentence about each one. For example:

They had cut the wedding cake.

5 Life changes

Malaysia has been independent for 40 years. Life used to be very different. Look at the pictures and read the information in the chart.

	Before independence	Today
Government	British colony	democracy
Main exports	timber, rubber, tin	electronic parts
School	often one child in family	all children
Work	many Malaysians worked abroad	full employment
Housing	old housing	modern housing
Economy	received aid from USA and Europe	gives aid to other countries

Kuala Lumpur, 1961

Kuala Lumpur, 2000

Write about the changes.

1 Before independence, Malaysia used to be a British colony. Now it is an independent democracy.

6 Around the world

Read about the black lemur in Madagascar. Choose the correct phrase to complete each sentence.

a is open only to scientists at the moment
b have studied the movements of the black lemurs for seven years
c bring noise and pollution with them
d only lives in north-west Madagascar
e is the fourth poorest country in the world
f is now common all over the world
g need the rainforest for agricultural land

The wild black lemur, which ¹_____, is in danger. One of the problems is that the islanders, who ²_____, are chopping down the trees in the rainforest. Madagascar, which ³_____, would like to bring more tourists to see its beautiful landscape. The Lokobe Rainforest Reserve, which ⁴_____, covers an area of 740 hectares. Research scientists, who ⁵_____, have discovered that they carry the seeds of trees from one part of the forest to the other. Tourists, who ⁶_____, might destroy the lemur and the forest. The problem in Madagascar, which ⁷_____, is how to balance the needs of the local people with the needs of the local wildlife.

Unit 3 Revision 15

Evaluation: Vocabulary

1 Looking at vocabulary

1.1 Vocabulary and you

Work by yourself. Answer the questions in the questionnaire. Compare your answers with other students.

1.2 Vocabulary in the classroom

Look back at the vocabulary you saw in Theme A. How did you learn the meaning of each word? Do you need to spend more time on vocabulary?

Write about your ideas and give your paper to your teacher. (You don't have to put your name on it.)

1.3 Be independent!
Improve your vocabulary!

Work in pairs or a small group. Brainstorm some ways you can develop your vocabulary.

How can you develop your vocabulary? For example: reading short stories, listening to …
How can you get more vocabulary practice? For example: making gap exercises, making a 'word bag', …
How can you help yourselves to remember new vocabulary? For example: making 'word maps', making posters for the classroom, …

Tell your teacher your ideas. Agree when you can do it, in class or at home.

Questionnaire
Vocabulary

Choose an answer, a, b, c or d.

1 If you see a lot of new words in class, do you practise them at home?
- ☐ **a** Always.
- ☐ **b** Sometimes.
- ☐ **c** Never.

2 If you have a vocabulary test, what do you do?
- ☐ **a** I don't do anything special.
- ☐ **b** I make wordlists and try to learn them.
- ☐ **c** I put words on cards and test myself.
- ☐ **d** Other:

3 What do you do to help yourself learn vocabulary?
- ☐ **a** I don't do anything special.
- ☐ **b** I make 'word maps' around a topic.
- ☐ **c** I read a lot.
- ☐ **d** Other:

4 If you read or hear a word that you don't understand, what do you do?
- ☐ **a** I usually ignore it.
- ☐ **b** I try to guess what it means.
- ☐ **c** I look it up in a dictionary.
- ☐ **d** Other:

Theme B
Visions of the future

1 Your vision of the future

Have you read or seen any stories about the future? What happens in each story? Do you think they are believable?
Have you read or heard anything about changes in the future? How will they affect *your* life?
Tell the class what you think.

2 Take a look at Theme B

Look at the pictures. Where can you find them in Units 4-6 and Option B?
Look at the descriptions of each Unit. In which unit or units can you:
- get help in finding the right job for you?
- learn some grammar?
- talk about protecting friends?
- learn about future predictions?
- use your imagination?

Around the Theme

UNIT

4 TOPIC AND LANGUAGE
Our future
page 18

What will life be like in the future? Read about some predictions for the year 2050. You can also learn how to use the Future perfect tense.

5 TOPIC AND LANGUAGE
After school
page 22

What job interests you most? Answer a questionnaire to find the right job for you. You can also learn about phrasal verbs in English and listen to someone talking about why they changed jobs.

6 OUT AND ABOUT
What should you do?
page 26

Lin doesn't know what to do. What is more important: keeping a secret or helping a friend with a problem. What do you think?

OPTION B FLUENCY
Write a story
page 80

Imagine... another place, another time, another world...use your imagination and create a story!

The future; revision of Future tenses, Future perfect; curriculum links with Science, Environmental Studies, Social Studies

1 *Discussion*

2 *Listening*
WB Ex. 1

3 *Discussion and reading*
IT A and B

Inside the text
A *Comprehension*
B *Vocabulary*

4 Our future
Topic and language

1 Thinking about the future

1.1 The image in your mind

What picture do you have of the future? What things will change? What things will happen?

Where do you see images of the future? Do you believe them?

Will life in the future be better, worse or the same as now? What do you *hope* about the future?

1.2 But when … ?

How quickly will things change?

Write down four of the things that you talked about in Exercise 1.1. When do you think they will happen? Write a date for each one. Compare with other students in the class.

Where can you see the beginnings of those changes *now*?

2 Studying the future

Futurologists are people who study the present and then try to predict the future. How do they do it, do you think?

Adriana Lima is a futurologist. She is telling Lars Bengtson about her work. Listen. Why is futurology important? What two types of futurology does she talk about?

3 The year 2050

3.1 Your predictions

In the year 2050, how old will you be?

What will life be like then, do you think? How will we live? Brainstorm predictions with the class.

Why do you predict *those* things?

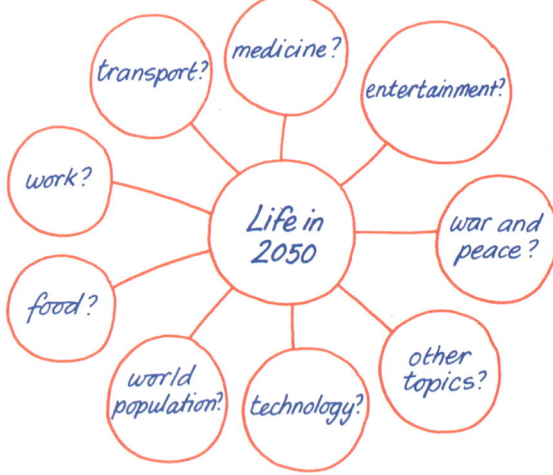

3.2 Futurologists' predictions

Futurologists predict that life will probably be very different in 2050. Read some of their predictions. Which ones do you think are good things? Which ones are bad? Which ones could be good *or* bad?

What do you think we should do *now* to make sure that only the good things happen?

18   Our future

BY 2050...

ENTERTAINMENT

TV channels will have disappeared. Instead, people will choose a programme from a 'menu' and a computer will send the programme directly to the television. Today, we can use the World Wide Web to read newspaper stories and see pictures on a computer thousands of kilometres away. By 2050, music, films, programmes, newspapers, and books will come to us by computer.

'Holographic Feedback TV' will have arrived. Holograms are pictures that have height, width and depth. Simple holograms exist today and 'virtual reality' games are already popular. By 2050, we will be able to see, smell and touch the things that we see on television.

THE ENVIRONMENT

Water will have become one of our most serious problems. In many places, agriculture is changing and they are growing fruit and vegetables to export. This uses a lot of water. Demand for water will increase ten times between now and 2050 and there could be serious shortages. Some futurologists predict that water could be the cause of war if we don't act now.

TRANSPORT

Cars will run on new, clean fuels and they will go very fast. Cars will have computers to control the speed of the car and there won't be any accidents. Today, many cars have computers that tell drivers exactly where they are. By 2050, the computer will control the car and drive it to your destination.

Space planes will take people halfway around the world in 2 hours. Today, the United States Space Shuttle can go into space and land on Earth again. By 2050, space planes will fly all over the world and people will fly from Los Angeles to Tokyo in just two hours.

TECHNOLOGY

Robots will have replaced people in factories. Many factories already use robots. Big companies prefer robots – they don't ask for pay rises or go on strike, and they work 24 hours a day. By 2050, we will see robots everywhere – in factories, schools, offices, hospitals, shops and homes.

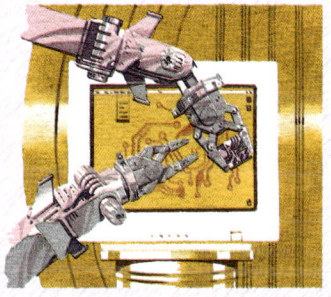

MEDICINE

Medical technology will have conquered many diseases. Today, there are electronic devices that connect directly to the brain to help people hear. By 2050, we will be able to help blind and deaf people to see and hear again.

Scientists will have discovered how to control genes. Scientists have already produced clones of animals. By 2050, scientists will be able to produce clones of people, and decide how they look, how they behave and how much intelligence they have. Scientists will be able to do these things – but should they?

Inside the text

A Check your understanding

What do the underlined pronouns refer to?

1. We will be able to see, smell and touch <u>them</u>.
2. <u>They</u> will take people halfway around the world in 2 hours.
3. <u>They</u> will be able to decide how <u>they</u> look and how much intelligence <u>they</u> have.
4. <u>It</u> could be the cause of war.

Now write four more sentences. Underline the pronouns and give the sentences to other students. Ask them what the pronouns refer to.

B What's the word?

Match each word to the correct meaning.

1. clone (n.)
2. gene (n.)
3. shortage (n.)
4. fuel (n.)
5. cause (n.)
6. prefer (v.)
7. conquer (v.)
8. predict (v.)
9. connect (v.)

a. defeat
b. like one thing more than another
c. join
d. say what will happen in the future
e. chemical 'information' in your body
f. an exact copy of an animal or thing
g. an amount that is not enough
h. something that gives heat or power
i. reason

Unit 4 · Topic and language   19

- 4 *Discussion and writing*
- 5 *'will' and 'going to'* WB Ex. 2
- 6 *Future perfect* WB Ex. 3
- 7 *Language Record*

4 From the present to the future

If the predictions are correct, then the world will change a lot. In your group, choose some predictions from Exercise 3.2. What will be the *effect* of each one?

Make an idea map and explain your ideas to the class. For example:

'Cars will run on new, clean fuels and they will go very fast.'

- People will travel a lot more.
  - There will be roads everywhere.
- People won't live near the place where they work.
  - Towns and villages will be 'dead'.
- There won't be so much pollution. The air will be cleaner.
  - People will be healthier.

Life in 2050?

5 Language focus
Revision: the future

5.1 Ways to talk about the future

There are many ways to talk about the future in English.

a You can use 'will' to talk about predictions.

Robots will travel into space in the next century.

b You can use 'going to' to talk about plans …

I'm going to meet my friend tomorrow.

… and about things that you think are certain to happen.

Look! Those cars are going to crash!

c You can also use the Present continuous to talk about fixed plans, especially with a definite time.

I'm playing football on Saturday.

Look at these sentences. Decide if you think they are predictions, plans or things certain to happen. Then complete each sentence with 'be going to' or 'will'.

1 I .... see a film tomorrow night.
2 I think I .... pass the English test tomorrow.
3 Alma .... study medicine when she leaves school.
4 Try this cake. You .... like it!
5 Many scientists say the climate .... change a lot in the next hundred years.
6 Look at the clouds! It .... rain.

5.2 Will or won't?

Complete these sentences with your own ideas about the future. Use 'will' or 'won't'. What do other students think?

1 Many people .... have enough to eat.
2 The Earth .... be very different.
3 There .... be a world government.
4 People .... live on another planet.
5 There .... be only one language in the world.
6 We .... eat the same things that we eat now.

20   Our future

6 Language focus Future perfect

6.1 In your language

How do you say these sentences in your language? They are examples of the Future perfect.

> By 2050, TV channels *will have disappeared*.
> Holographic TV *will have arrived*.

Can you find some more examples in Exercise 3?

6.2 How to form the Future perfect

You can use the Future perfect to talk about something that *will have been completed in the future*. You form it with 'will' and the Present perfect ('have' and the past participle).

Can you complete this table? (For irregular verbs, see page 90.)

Infinitive	Present perfect	Future perfect
be	have been	will have been
arrive		
become		
conquer		
disappear		
discover		
grow		
increase		
reach		
rise		

6.3 Some more predictions

Here is some information about the world today. How do you think things will change? Write a sentence about each one.

1 Today, the world's population is about 5 billion. By 2050, it *will have reached 10 billion*.

2 China has the largest population, with 1.2 billion. By 2050, …

3 India has a smaller population than China, but by 2050, India …

4 At the moment, we use 2,400 cubic kilometres of water a year but this is growing very fast. By the year 2050, it …

5 Some scientists say that the temperature of the Earth is rising 0.1°C every year because of pollution. By 2050, they say …

6 The rise in temperature is melting the ice at the North and South Poles and the sea level is rising. Compared to the sea level in 1970, some scientists say that by 2010 …

You can check your ideas on page 90.

7 Your Language Record

7.1 Your Grammar Record

Make notes in your *Grammar Record* about how to form and use the Future perfect. Look at Exercise 6 and the *Language summaries* in your Workbook for ideas.

7.2 Your Record of Language Use

Look back at the Unit. Are there more words or phrases you want to add to your *Record of Language Use*? Check with this list.

Nouns accident amount brain cause demand depth destination device disease driver fuel height hologram menu pay rise prediction programme shortage speed strike virtual reality width

Verbs act connect clone conquer exist land predict prefer smell touch

Adjectives blind deaf popular serious

Adverbs directly exactly halfway

Time to spare?

Choose one of these exercises.

1 Look at the *Help yourself list* on pages 91–2. Make an exercise about this Unit.

2 What do you think will happen in your school in the next two weeks? Write some predictions, put them in an envelope and look at them after 15 days.

> I predict that on Monday … will …

3 Think about the place where you live. How will it have changed 50 years from now? Write a few sentences about your ideas. You can think about the roads, the houses, the shops, the buildings, the trees and plants, the traffic, and the people.

> I think that in 50 years from now …

Your personal future; jobs in the future; phrasal verbs

1. *Discussion*
2. *Reading*
3. *Reading and analysing*
   WB Ex. 1

5 After school
Topic and language

1 Talents and interests

What hobbies or interests do you have?

Do you like doing these things? Put a tick (✓) to show your answer. Compare with your neighbour.

	a lot	only sometimes	very little
• reading or writing stories and letters			
• learning facts about the world			
• mending things or seeing how they work			
• drawing, painting or making music			
• helping people or looking after children			
• planning or organising things			

Are there some subjects at school that you like a lot? Tell the class what you think.

2 After school

2.1 Your ideas

Do you have any ideas about what job you would like to do when you leave school? What decisions do you have to take *now* to prepare yourself? Which jobs would you definitely *not* like to do? Tell the class what you think.

2.2 Different jobs, different interests

Often it is very difficult to decide what you want to do. By yourself, complete the questionnaire on page 23. Follow the instructions carefully. Read about the different types of jobs.

Does the questionnaire help you decide what you would like to do?

3 Some more jobs

Most jobs are a combination of different things. For example, if you are an actor you are *working with language* but you are also doing *creative work*.

Look at the six types of jobs again. What things are involved in these jobs?

doctor   gardener   librarian   painter
politician   swimming teacher   taxi driver
TV news presenter

WHAT'S THE RIGHT JOB FOR YOU?

STEP 1

Look at the circles. First, compare the jobs in Circle A with the jobs in Circle B. Which group of jobs attracts you more? You have three points to give. For example, you could give Circle A two points and Circle B one point, or you could give Circle A zero points and Circle B three points. The total must be 3. Write the number of points in the boxes on the line from Circle A to Circle B. Continue in the same way so that you compare all the circles.

22   After school

STEP 2

Add up the points for each circle. Draw a graph to show the total for each circle. Now read about the circles that you gave the highest points.

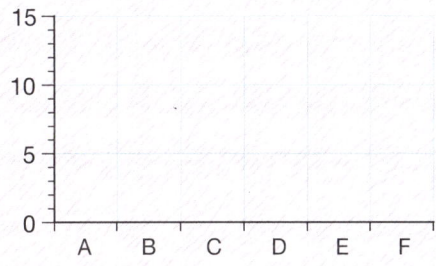

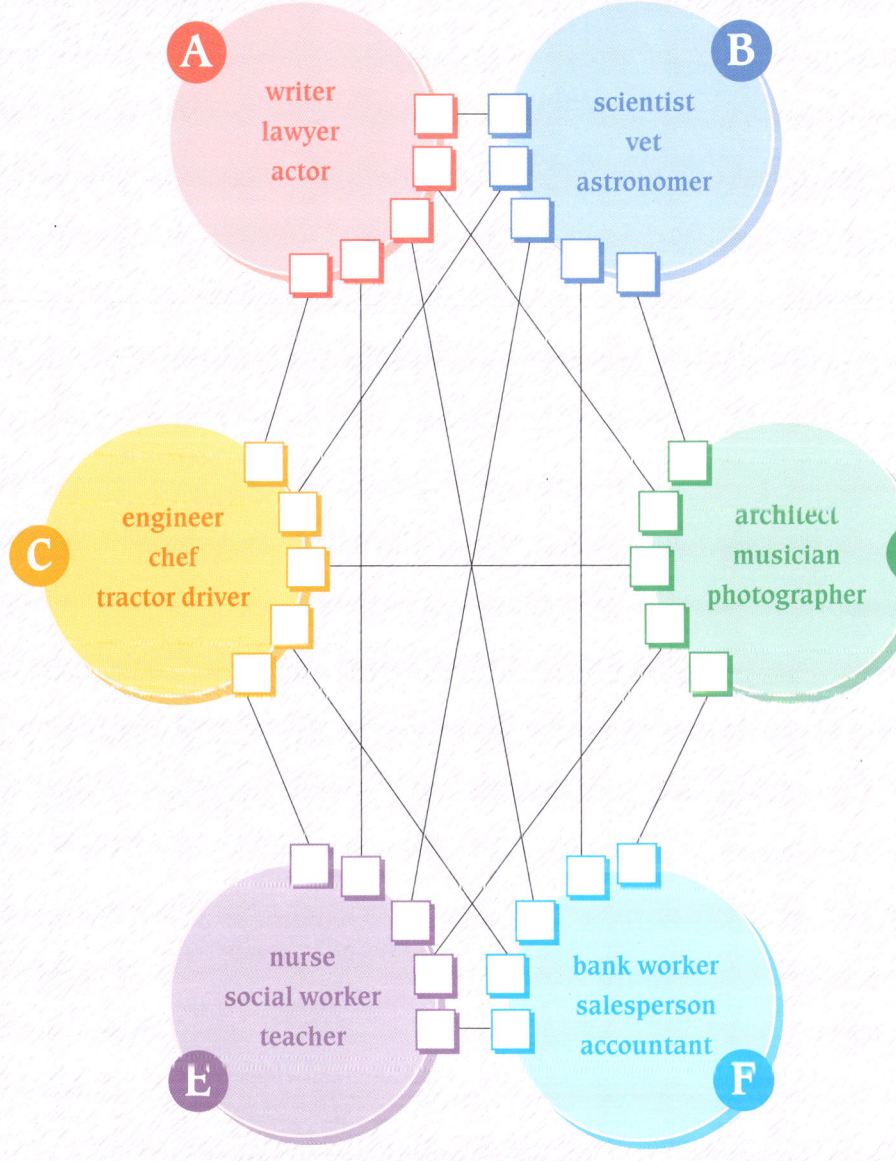

Circle A: *Working with language*
You enjoy working with ideas and communicating. You probably also enjoy reading and like writing things down – especially when you are thinking about something.

Circle B: *Science and research*
You enjoy knowing things. You like finding things out, perhaps by looking things up in books, by working things out or by experimenting.

Circle C: *Practical work*
You enjoy doing things with your hands. You enjoy constructing things or perhaps repairing things. You are not happy just sitting down – you like being physically active.

Circle D: *Creative work*
You enjoy expressing your ideas – but not so much with words. You like creating things that people can see or hear.

Circle E: *Social work*
You enjoy helping other people. You need a lot of patience because it is often difficult to help people.

Circle F: *Administrative work*
You like organising and planning things. You don't like taking too many risks, and you prefer things to be clear. Precise facts and information are important to you.

23

4 *Phrasal verbs*
WB Ex. 2;
TB Ws. 5

5 *Listening*

6 *Writing*

7 *Language Record*
WB Ex. 2,
Vocabulary Map 1

4 Language focus Phrasal verbs

4.1 One-word and two-word verbs

Most verbs in English are just one word. For example:

go   say   buy   enjoy

However, there are also a lot of two-word verbs. These are called 'phrasal verbs'. For example:

get up   write down   turn on   turn off

Look back at the questionnaire in Exercise 2. Can you find six more examples? How do you say those verbs in your language?

4.2 What's the phrasal verb?

Can you complete each of these sentences with the correct phrasal verb from the list?

add up   find out   get up   look up   sit down
turn off   turn on   write down

a With a pen or pencil, you can .... your ideas.
b If you want to telephone somebody, you can .... their number in a telephone directory.
c Can you .... the light? I want to go to sleep.
d What time do you .... in the morning?
e Come in and ....
f An encyclopaedia can help you .... many things about the world.
g .... the radio. I want to hear the news.
h A calculator can help you .... numbers.

4.3 How can you learn phrasal verbs?

Often, it is difficult to remember the meaning of a phrasal verb. With some verbs, the extra word only changes the meaning a little. For example:

write – write down   sit – sit down

With other verbs, it gives a very different meaning.

get   get up (in the morning)
look   look up (a word in a dictionary)

There isn't any 'system' – and there is only one way to remember the meaning of phrasal verbs: learn them when you see or hear them!

4.4 Be careful!

Notice how you can say an object pronoun with a phrasal verb.

Write down *this number* → Write *it* down.

Where does the pronoun go? Can you change these sentences in the same way?

a Turn off *the radio and television*, please.
b Can you turn on *the light*, please?
c He looked up *the numbers* in the telephone directory.
d She added up *the prices* with a calculator.
e Can you find out *the population of England*?

5 Changing jobs

Many people have to change to a completely different job because they cannot find work. Listen to Rafael Ortega from Mexico. He is talking to Liz Simpson about why he changed his job.

a What job did he train to do?
b Why couldn't he find work?
c What does he do now?
d How are his old job and his new job similar?

24   After school

6 Jobs for the future

6.1 In your lifetime

Probably in your lifetime you will have many different jobs. Things will change very quickly and you will have to change also. Look back at what you read and talked about in Unit 4. How will work change in the future, do you think?

Tell the class your ideas.

6.2 New jobs

Probably some jobs will disappear completely and new jobs will appear. Choose three or four jobs that people do now. How will those jobs change in the future? What new jobs will appear? Work with your neighbour or in a small group and make some notes. For example:

> Librarian
> Perhaps people won't read books in the future. They will read, hear and see everything on a computer.
> SO: We will need people to organise and choose the things to put on the computers.

You could make a poster of your ideas.

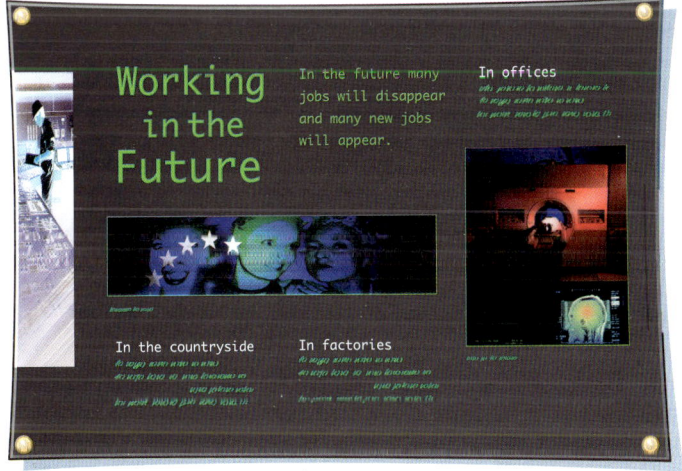

7 Your Language Record

7.1 Your Grammar Record

Make notes in your *Grammar Record* about phrasal verbs. Write down some examples. Look at Exercise 4 and the *Language summaries* in your Workbook for ideas.

7.2 Your Record of Language Use

Look back at the Unit. Are there more words or phrases you want to add to your *Record of Language Use*? Check with this list.

Nouns *Names of jobs*: accountant actor architect astronomer bank worker chef doctor engineer gardener lawyer librarian musician nurse painter photographer politician salesperson scientist social worker taxi driver teacher tractor driver TV news presenter vet writer
Other nouns: total graph patience risk

Verbs attract construct create experiment express prefer
Phrasal verbs: add up find out look up turn off turn on work out

Adjectives active precise

Adverbs especially physically

Time to spare?

Choose one of these exercises.

1 Look at the *Help yourself list* on pages 91-2. Make an exercise about this Unit.

2 Choose two or three jobs. What do you have to *do* in each job? What do you think you have to *learn* to do in each job? Make a list of your ideas. Later, ask people and find out if you are correct.

3 Look at Unit 4 again. Think about two or three new jobs in the future. What do you think people will have to do in each job? Write a description.

Unit 5 Topic and language   25

Obligations and friendship; helping someone against their will

1. *Discussion*
2. *Listening and discussion*
3. *Conditionals*
4. a *Writing and speaking*
   b *Writing*
   c *You decide*

6 What should you do?
Out and about with English

1 What do you think?

Discuss these questions with your class.

If you know that a friend is doing something wrong, what should you do? Does it depend on what it is? Does it depend on who it is? Does it depend on whether it hurts someone else?

What should you do in these situations?

a You know that a friend never does his/her schoolwork.
b You know that a friend often steals things from a shop.
c You know that a friend is going to run away from home.

2 The right thing to do

2.1 Lin's problem

Listen to Part A of the conversation. Discuss these questions with a neighbour, and then tell the class what you think.

Why is Lin worried?
Do you think Lin has a good reason to worry?
Is it right that she tells Otis about Sarah?

2.2 Charlotte's and Otis's opinions

Listen to Part B. Note down your ideas to these questions and then find out what other students think.

Do you think Charlotte 'has a point'?
Is Otis right when he says 'it's her life'?
What is more important – Sarah's trust in Lin, or Sarah's health?
Do you think Sarah should tell someone?

2.3 Promises …

Listen to Part C.

Why does Lin say 'Otis, you promised!'?
Do you think Otis is doing the right thing?

3 Inside the text
Conditionals

In Part A there are two conditional sentences:

Giving advice: If you want to help her, you have to tell someone.
Describing possible results: If I did that, she would never trust me again.

Complete these sentences with your own ideas.

a If you want to play the guitar well, you have to …
b If you want to travel, you …
c If you want to learn English, …
d If I lost my school books, …
e If I fell from a window, …
f If I broke my leg, …

4 Decide …

Work by yourself or in a small group. Choose a, b or c.

a What happened next?

Did Otis tell Mr Harper? What did Mr Harper say? What happened? Prepare a conversation with Mr Harper. Act it out for the class.

b Smoking kills!

Design some posters to tell students about the dangers of smoking. You can give some reasons for not starting or some advice on how to stop.

c You decide!

Look at pages 91–2 for ideas. You could:

– make an exercise about this Unit.
– write a poem about a friend or about smoking.
– prepare and act out a conversation about a friend.

26   What should you do?

Lin's problem

Part A

OTIS: Hi, Lin. What's up?
LIN: I'm thinking. I'm worried about someone.
OTIS: Who?
LIN: I can't tell you.
OTIS: Well, what's the problem?
LIN: Well, um, I've got a friend … and he or she needs help … but he or she … won't let me help him or her.
OTIS: I don't follow!
LIN: Do you promise you won't tell anyone?
OTIS: Cross my heart.
LIN: It's Sarah. She's started smoking – a lot. Sometimes she smokes about 30 cigarettes a day.
OTIS: She'll grow out of it.
LIN: I don't think so. She's only fifteen and it's already a habit. I'm worried.

Part B

CHARLOTTE: Hi, Lin. Hi, Otis. What are you talking about?
OTIS: Lin's got a friend who's smoking a lot.
CHARLOTTE: How old is he?
LIN: *She's* fifteen.
CHARLOTTE: That's illegal.
LIN: No, it's not. Anyway, that's not the point.
CHARLOTTE: Yes it is. She's not allowed to buy cigarettes.
OTIS: Doesn't she know it's bad for her?
LIN: Of course. She says she can stop when she wants to stop.
OTIS: Well, it's her life.
LIN: That's an easy way out, Otis.
OTIS: She should talk to someone about it.
LIN: That's what I say but she won't listen.
OTIS: Well, why don't you tell one of the teachers?
LIN: I can't do that! She's my friend. She trusts me.

Part C

CHARLOTTE: Lin, if you want to help her, you have to tell someone.
LIN: If I did that, she would never trust me again.
OTIS: Well, *I* can tell someone.
LIN: No, Otis.
CHARLOTTE: Look, you want to help her, right?
LIN: Yes.
MR HARPER: Hello, you three. What are you doing?
LIN: Nothing, Mr Harper.
OTIS: We're talking. Mr Harper, can you help us?
LIN: Otis, you promised!
MR HARPER: What did you promise, Otis?
OTIS: Well, Lin's got a friend who …

Idiom box

What's up? What's the problem?
I don't follow I don't understand
Cross my heart. I promise completely.
grow out of something become older and lose interest in it

Unit 6 Out and about with English

Evaluation | Writing

1 Looking at writing

1.1 Writing and you

Work by yourself. Answer the questions. Compare your answers with other students in your class.

1.2 Writing in the classroom

Look back at the writing you did in Theme A and B.
What problems did you have?
Was it difficult or easy to write?
Did you enjoy it? Why/why not?
How can you improve your work next time?
Write about your ideas and give your paper to your teacher. (You don't have to put your name on it.)

1.3 Be independent!
Improve your writing!

Work in pairs or a small group. Brainstorm some ways you can get extra writing practice.

What can you write? For example: posters, letters, stories, poems …
What can you write about? For example: the environment, your life, your town …
How can you write? For example, alone, in pairs, in a small group …
How can you do it? For example, brainstorm ideas first, make notes, then write in rough, then …

Tell your teacher your ideas. Agree when you can do it, in class or at home.

Questionnaire
Writing

1 When you have to write something in English, do you:
- ☐ a start writing immediately?
- ☐ b make notes first?
- ☐ c read something first?
- ☐ d do something else?

2 While you are writing, do you:
- ☐ a check everything while you write?
- ☐ b check everything after you have finished?
- ☐ c check only the things you aren't sure about?
- ☐ d check nothing?

3 While you are writing, do you:
- ☐ a leave plenty of space to make changes?
- ☐ b cross things out with a single line?
- ☐ c cross things out completely?
- ☐ d do something else?

4 When you have finished, do you:
- ☐ a read what you have written and make changes?
- ☐ b make a 'clean' copy of your work?
- ☐ c close your book immediately?

Theme C — Media stories

1 The news and you

Work in a small group. Find out how everyone finds out about the news, for example: newspaper, radio, internet.

Now write some questions as part of a class questionnaire to find out what people in your school think about the news. You can ask, for example:

- how much time people spend getting news
- when they get it
- what they think about the quality of the reports
- which are the most important news stories
- which are their favourite news stories

Share your ideas with the class and make one or two questionnaires. Ask as many people as you can to complete the questionnaire.

2 Take a look a Theme C

Look at the pictures. Where can you find them in Units 7–9 and Option C?
Look at the descriptions of each Unit. In which unit or units can you:

- learn some grammar?
- learn about how television can affect us?
- find out about the American people?
- hear journalists choosing news stories?
- read some news stories?

Around the Theme

UNIT

7 TOPIC AND LANGUAGE
The magic box
page 30

Television is a wonderful! It's great to watch – what are your favourite programmes? Television can also be bad – read about how it can affect us and our lives. You can also revise the use of the Present perfect and the Past simple.

8 TOPIC AND LANGUAGE
The news
page 34

What types of stories become the main news? How do journalists choose news stories? Find out in Unit 8. You can also learn how to use question tags in English.

9 ALL ABOUT... The news
What should you do?
page 38

A fire in Mongolia ... lost on Mount Everest ... new dinosaurs ... Read some news stories from around the world.

OPTION C CULTURE MATTERS
The USA – a melting pot
page 91

Who lives in the USA? The USA has one of the most mixed populations in the world. Find out where everyone came from in Option C.

Watching television; the effects of television; Present perfect and Past simple; curriculum links with Social Studies

1 *Discussion and writing*

2 *Listening*
WB Ex. 1

3 *Discussion and reading*

7 The magic box
Topic and language

1 On television

1.1 The programmes you like

What are your favourite television programmes? Do you like particular *types* of programmes? What types of programmes don't you like? Tell the class your ideas.

1.2 When do you watch TV?

When do you usually watch TV? How long do you watch, do you think? Do you normally do something else while you are watching TV?

Work by yourself and complete the table. Compare with other students in your class.

Television habits

Time	How long?	Other activities?
During the week morning 6 am–12 pm		
afternoon 12 pm–6 pm		
early evening 6 pm–9 pm		
late evening/night 9 pm+		
At the weekend morning 6 am–12 pm		
afternoon 12 pm–6 pm		
early evening 6 pm–9 pm		
late evening/night 9 pm+		

2 Television schedules

How do TV stations decide when to show different programmes, do you think?

Are most television stations in your country commercial? Does that affect the programmes they show, do you think?

📼 Sue Brown works in a TV station. Mel Ford asked her how TV stations decide when to show the different programmes. Listen to the first part of their conversation.

What type of programmes do they show in the morning and after half past three? Why?
What is 'prime time'?
Is it the same in your country?

📼 Listen to the next part of their conversation.

How are programmes before and after 9 pm different?
Do you think it is necessary to have that difference?
What are 'ratings'?
How does a TV company find out its ratings?
Why are they important?

3 The effects of television

3.1 Good and bad

Television has changed our lives in many ways. It has brought many positive things but also many negative things. Work in a small group or with your neighbour. Think hard! Add as many points as you can to the two lists.

> THE EFFECTS OF TELEVISION
> Positive   Negative
> You can learn a lot.   It takes a lot of your time.

3.2 Television research

Read about some of the research into the effects of television. Does the article mention any of your points from Exercise 3.1?

THE MAGIC BOX

TELEVISION has changed our lives in many ways. Many people now spend more time watching TV than doing anything else. Researchers in the USA have estimated that when most students leave school they have spent 11,000 hours in the classroom and 22,000 hours watching television. But what effect does this have?

Benefits of television

- Television helps us to learn more about the world and to know and see many new things. Television can often present information to us in a more effective way than books can. It can also make things more memorable.

- It entertains us. It is an enjoyable way to relax. For millions of people around the world, television is a source of companionship and helps them to cope with everyday life.

- It has increased the popularity of sports and arts.

- It has made us aware of our global responsibilities. In 1985, for example, 1.5 billion people in 147 countries watched a TV pop concert and helped to collect more than $100 million for people in Africa.

Dangers

- Television can make us passive. We don't have to think and our brains become lazy.

- It encourages us to buy things that we don't need, and can make us unhappy with our own lives.

- It takes time away from activities such as reading, conversation, and games.

- It gives a false picture of society. A study in 1991 showed that people who watch a lot of television are more afraid of crime. They also think that there is a lot more crime than there really is.

- Some critics say that television makes people violent. A ten-year study in the United States showed that children who watch violent television programmes are more likely to be violent themselves.

3.3 What can we do?

Work in a small group or with your neighbour. Look back at the 'negative' points you made in Exercise 3.1 and the 'dangers' listed in the text. What can we do about them? Make a list of your ideas. You could make a class poster.

Unit 7 Topic and language

4 *Past simple and Present perfect*
WB Ex. 3
TB Ws. 7

5 *Language Record*
WB Ex. 2

4 Language focus
Past simple and Present perfect

4.1 Remember?

In Exercise 3 you saw sentences like these:

> Television *has changed* our lives in many ways. It *has made* us aware of our global responsibilities.

You also saw sentences like this:

> In 1985, 1.5 billion people *watched* a TV pop concert and *helped* to collect more than $100 million for people in Africa.

Do you remember the names of the different forms of the verb? Do you remember when you use them? Discuss this with your neighbour and tell the class.

Look back at the text in Exercise 3.2. Can you find any more examples of each form?

4.2 Past actions and present results

The two types of verb forms in Exercise 4.1 are called 'Present perfect' and 'Past simple'. Can you match each description to the correct verb form?

a You can use this verb form to talk about an action in the past that has a result now or that includes a 'now' time (today, this week, never).

b You can use this verb form to talk about an action at a definite time in the past that does not include 'now'.

Are these sentences examples of the Past simple or the Present perfect? Write 'a' or 'b' for each sentence and the name of the verb form.

1 My mother lived in Spain before she got married.
2 I've never read a complete book in English.
3 Scientists have discovered life on Mars!
4 They discovered a new planet, Pluto, in 1930.
5 Have you read the newspaper today?
6 Did you pass your test last week?
7 Dinosaurs disappeared 63 million years ago.
8 Oh, no! I've forgotten my book.

4.3 Past simple or Present perfect?

Would you use the Past simple or the Present perfect with these time words?

a today b last Thursday c never
d this year e in 1997 f in my life
g when I was five years old

Now complete these sentences with the correct form of the verb. Look at the list on page 90 for irregular verbs.

1 Jack .... (do) a lot today. He .... (write) three letters and .... (read) a book.
2 We .... (go) to the cinema last Thursday. The film .... (be) very good.
3 I .... (never, see) a ghost.
4 They .... (increase) the price of bus tickets twice this year.
5 In 1997, Pathfinder .... (send) pictures back from the planet Mars.
6 I .... (live) in three different countries in my life.
7 I .... (start) school when I was five years old.

4.4 Television news

Notice how you can use the Present perfect to give news and the Past simple to give more details.

A The Presidents of the USA and Russia have signed a new agreement.
B Where did they sign it?
A They signed it in New York.

a

USA and Russia: a new trade agreement.
New York

Work with a partner. Imagine that one of you saw these news stories on television last night. Tell the news to your partner, who should ask for more details:

Where …?   When …?   Who …?   How much …?   How fast?

b — New dinosaur bones. Peru
c — Landing on Venus. 03:15
d — Plane crash: no deaths. Switzerland
e — Steve Winston: a new world record. 2 km in 3 minutes
f — Mexico. 23.20

4.5 More news

What stories have you seen on the television recently? Think for a few moments and write a few sentences. Use the Present perfect and then the Past simple. Tell the class.

5 Your Language Record

5.1 Your Grammar Record

Make notes in your *Grammar Record* about the differences between the Past simple and the Present perfect, and add some examples. Look at Exercise 4 and the *Language summaries* in your Workbook for ideas.

5.2 Your Record of Language Use

Look back at the Unit. Are there more words or phrases you want to add to your *Record of Language Use*? Check with this list.

Nouns crime popularity prime time rating research researcher responsibility

Verbs encourage entertain estimate relax

Adjectives afraid commercial enjoyable false global lazy passive unhappy violent

Time to spare?
Choose one of these exercises.

1 Look at the *Help yourself list* on pages 91–2. Make an exercise about this Unit.

2 Think about a programme that you like. What is it about? What happened in the programme the last time you saw it? Write a paragraph or two to describe it.

3 You can talk about your experiences in the same way as you can talk about the news. For example:

   I've been to five big cities. I went to … in …

   Answer these questions and give more details.

   How many big cities have you been to in your life?
   How many times have you been on a plane/train/boat?
   How many films have you seen this month?
   How many drinks have you had today?
   How many books have you read this year?

Unit 7 Topic and language 33

News media; curriculum links with Media and Communication Studies; question tags

1 *Discussion*
WB Ex. 1

2 *Reading*
IT A and B

Inside the text
A *Vocabulary*
B *Discourse*

8 The news
Topic and language

1 Think about the news

How do you get to know the news? Do you watch the news on TV? Do you listen to the news on the radio? Do you read a newspaper regularly? Do you think the news is interesting?

2 What is news?

2.1 News stories

Read these newspaper headlines. Which stories do you think should be on the TV news? Why? Why not? Which types of stories should be the main news?

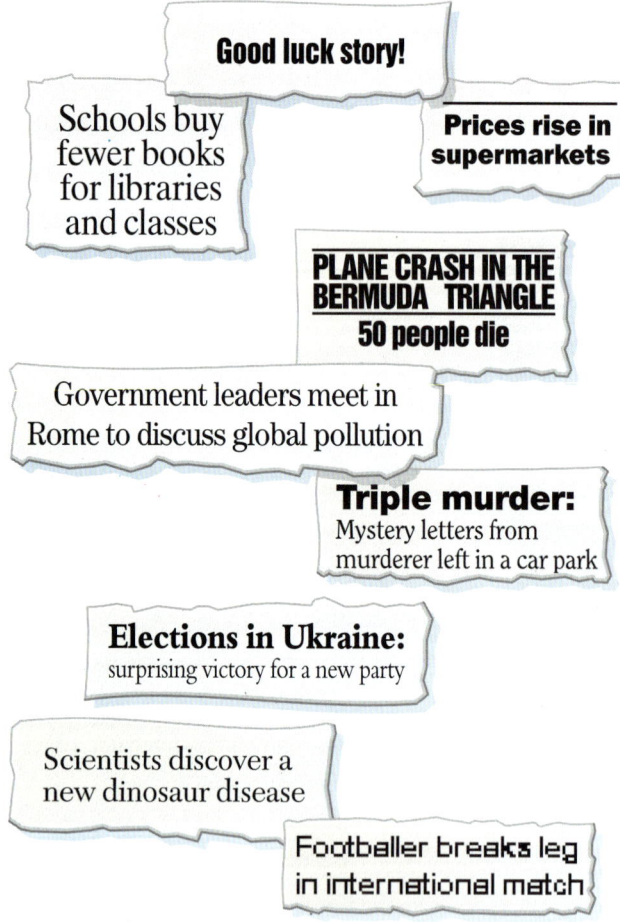

2.2 What's in the news?

Here are some of the main types of stories on the TV news. Can you match each story from Exercise 2.1 to the correct type?

politics   crime   foreign news   science
home news: personal stories   economics
home news: serious   sport

Do you have the same types of news stories in your country?

3 What's in the news?

3.1 Is the news interesting?

Read the advertisement. What do you think? How can television companies make the news more interesting for young people?

THE YOUNG PERSONS NEWS AWARD
The *Young Persons News Award* is open to all students between 12 and 15 years old. We are looking for comments, suggestions, analysis and criticism of all news broadcasts.
How can we make news broadcasts more interesting for young people?
Please send your ideas as entries to the competition.
Prizes: A chance to produce your own news broadcast, and to spend a day with news journalists.
Closing date: 20 December
Send entries to

3.2 The news award

Read about the Young Persons News Award. Do the reports mention your ideas? How many ideas for improving the news can you find in the texts?

Is the information in the reports also true for your country?

34 The news

EDUCATION NEWS ROUNDUP
The Young Persons News Award

Students from schools all around the country entered the Young Persons News Award this year. Here are some extracts from their reports on the daily news broadcasts.

Report 1

For our report we watched twenty thirty-minute news broadcasts over four weeks. We timed each kind of story.

We thought that news bulletins could spend more time on foreign news. It is not surprising that many people do not know what is happening in other parts of the world. At the moment foreign news reports are often superficial.

Pupils at High Hill School watched the news for four weeks

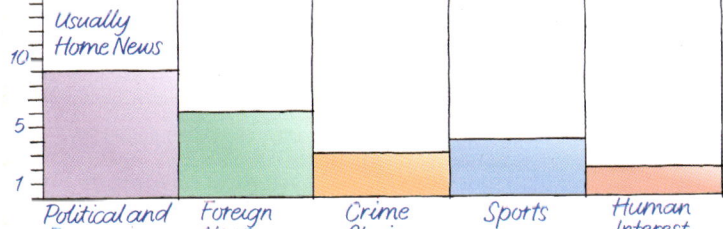

Report 2

We wanted to see how many news stories are about ordinary people. We looked at the human interest stories which are usually on before the sports stories.

We watched thirty news broadcasts. Twenty-four programmes had 'human interest' stories.

The stories were in three groups – tragic, happy and strange. The 'strange' group included stories about coincidences and mysteries.

In the 'tragic' group there were stories about children, accidents and illnesses. In the 'happy' group there were stories about people winning money or an unexpected recovery from illness. It is a good idea to have stories about real people. The problem is that these stories are 'gossip'. It would be better if the news had more reports about people who are working in science and industry.

Report 3

The last story on the news is usually about sports. We watched forty-two news programmes on different channels at different times of the day. We found that more than 85% of the sports stories were about football and more than 90% of them were about sportsmen not sportswomen. The sports news is too dominated by 'male' sports like football. This is very repetitive and boring

The students made some very useful suggestions about how news bulletins could be more interesting. Some suggested that there could be more 'good' news, that there could be more regional news, others suggested there could be 'themes' for a week – on science, space, the sea, etc. – or the news stories could be in a different sequence each day.

Inside the text

A Negative and positive

Look at the words in the box. Which words are negative? Which words are positive? Make two lists.

```
tragic   gossip   win   better   dominated
boring   repetitive   problem   recovery
accident   superficial   balanced
```

B Check your understanding

Find these sentences in the texts. In each one, is the writer positive, critical or neutral?

1 The last story on the news is usually about sports.
2 We wanted to see how many news stories are about ordinary people.
3 The sports news is too dominated by 'male' sports like football.
4 It is not surprising that many people do not know what is happening in other parts of the world.
5 We thought that news bulletins could spend more time on foreign news.

4 *Reading and listening*

5 *Question tags*
WB Ex. 2; TB Ws. 8

6 *Language Record*

4 Stories on the news

Gail Duncan is a chief news editor. Every morning she has a meeting with an assistant news editor, a producer and different correspondents. At the meeting they choose the news stories for the day.

🔊 Listen. Which seven stories do they choose?

Look back at the list of types of stories in Exercise 2.2. Which *type* of stories did they choose?

Why did they choose each story? Read this list of reasons and listen again. Match each reason to a story.

a People are worried about education. *Schools and books*
b It's about a very popular sports person.
c It's a political story and they have interviews with politicians.
d It's an unusual story and they have an interview on tape.
e It's a mysterious story.
f It's a good crime story.
g Everyone likes to hear about good luck.

5 Language focus Question tags

5.1 What do you say?

How do you say these sentences in your language?

He's a very popular footballer, *isn't he*?
We've got a lot of film of that, *haven't we*?

These are examples of 'question tags'. Read the sentences again. Why do you think we use them? Tell the class your ideas.

5.2 Different uses for question tags

We normally only use question tags when we are speaking (not writing). You can use question tags:

– if you expect people to agree with you
– if you want to check something

If you expect someone to agree, make your voice go down.

That was an interesting programme, wasn't it? ↘

If you want to check something, make your voice go up.

Her name's Jill, isn't it? ↗

🔊 Listen. Are the people expecting someone to agree or are they checking? Draw an arrow up or down.

It's very nice today, isn't it?
The new History teacher's nice, isn't she?
His name's Juan, isn't it?
You're from Brazil, aren't you?
You can come on Saturday, can't you?
This Maths homework isn't very hard, is it?

5.3 How to form question tags

Look at the question tags in Exercises 5.1 and 5.2 again. How can you make question tags? Match the two halves of the sentences to make a rule.

If the sentence is positive, …	… you use a positive question tag.
If the sentence is negative, …	… you use a negative question tag.

What verb and subject do you use in a question tag? Look at the sentences in Exercises 5.1 and 5.2 again. Tell the class your ideas and then check in the Workbook Language summaries.

36 The news

5.4 Other verbs

When the verb in the main sentence is an auxiliary or modal verb ('be', 'can', 'have', 'should', 'will', etc.) you use the same verb in the question tag. With all other verbs you use the verb 'do' in the question tag. Look:

Yes, everyone *likes* a mystery, *don't* they?

He usually *plays* football for England, *doesn't* he?

The archaeologist *doesn't say* who found the bones, *does* she?

We *don't have* discoveries like that every day, *do* we?

Can you complete the question tags in these sentences? Two bank guards are watching security television screens.

a Look! That's the bank manager, isn't it? He doesn't work at night, ... ?

No, he goes home at 5 o'clock, ... ?

b What's wrong with the dogs. They don't usually go to sleep, ... ?

No. Those dogs guard the back of the bank, ... ?

c Who are those two men? They look suspicious, ... ?

Yes. They've got something in their hands, ... ?

d Look. The manager is opening a door. The alarm bell rings if you open that door, ... ?

Well, I think he's got the key. He takes it home with him .... ? What's that? It looks like a gun, ... ?

e This doesn't look good, ... ?

No. Come on, let's find out what they're doing!

6 Your Language Record

6.1 Your Grammar Record

Make notes about questions tags in your *Grammar Record*. Make notes about how to form them and how to use them. Look at Exercise 5 and the Language summaries in your Workbook for ideas.

6.2 Your Record of Language Use

Look back at Unit 8. Are there more words and phrases you want to add to your *Record of Language Use*? Check your record with this list.

Nouns politics   economics   crime   extract   broadcasts   bulletins   coincidences   recovery   gossip   channel

Verbs time   suggest

Adjectives daily   foreign   home (news)   surprising   superficial   ordinary   tragic   dominated   repetitive

Time to spare?

Choose one of these exercises.

1 Look at the *Help yourself list* on pages 91–2. Make an exercise about this Unit.

2 Write a questionnaire to find out how students in your class spend their leisure time.

3 Choose one of the headlines in Ex2.1 and write the news story for a TV news report..

1 *Fluency*
2 a *Writing and speaking*
  b *You decide!*

9 ALL ABOUT...
The news

1 All about ... the news

1.1 Search!

Look at the titles of the news stories. (Don't read the stories yet.) Which story do you think will tell you about ...

a the work of international medical teams.
b how young people spend their time.
c new information about how the continents have moved.
d the weather in the Himalayas.

Read the texts and check your answers.

1.2 Key words

These are the key words from three sentences in the text about Mount Everest. Without looking at the text again, try to write the three sentences.

Sentence 1: Bob Chapman and Jessie Martin famous   missing   Mount Everest

Sentence 2: Chapman and Martin South Col camp   Sunday

Sentence 3: South Col   last camp before the peak

Compare your sentences with the texts. Write some more key words for other students.

2 Decide ...

Choose a or b

a Make your own TV news programme

Work in pairs or in a small group. You are a news team. You have to prepare the news for tonight's TV news broadcast. The programme is five minutes long.

Read the texts again. They are some of the main stories for the day. Decide which ones you will use. You can also use some stories from Exercise 2.1.

When you are ready, present your news programme to the class.

b Decide!

Decide what you want to do and ask your teacher. You could ...

– design a news programme for young people.
– prepare a news report about events in your school.
– prepare an interview with another student about a lucky experience.
– prepare a news report on a world event.

Look at the *Help yourself list* on page 91-2 for ideas.

Two climbers have disappeared on Mount Everest

Ben Chapman and Jessie Martin, the famous mountain climbers, are still missing on Mount Everest. Chapman and Martin left South Col camp on Sunday. South Col is the last camp on the mountain before the peak. All climbers know that they have to get up to the peak and back before the weather changes or before they have bad altitude sickness. The weather is very bad at the peak at the moment. (Film interview with Margaret Black, Everest climber.)

Fires in Mongolia

Fires are still spreading across Mongolia. This is the fourth week. Five thousand people have left their homes. Two hundred people have been killed or injured by fire and smoke and falling trees. One thousand square miles of forest have disappeared. The rivers are dry. The international medical teams, Red Cross and Medicins sans Frontières, are arriving with medical supplies. (Film of fires in Mongolia.)

New dinosaurs!

An international team has discovered the bones of two new species of dinosaurs in the Atlas mountains, Morocco. The dinosaurs lived more than 90 million years ago. One of the dinosaurs had very sharp teeth which shows that it ate meat.
'The most interesting thing about this dinosaur is that it is similar to a dinosaur that another team found in Argentina last year,' said Angela Milner from the Natural History Museum. 'This tells us a lot about how the continents used to be connected and when they started to break up.'

Teenage survey!

The government has just completed an investigation into how teenagers in Britain spend their free time. 1,600 teenage children at 67 different schools answered a questionnaire on spare time activities, homework, pocket money, friends, family life, the future, examinations, holidays, favourite books, TV programmes and music. Their answers will be interesting to all parents and teachers. The Channel 8 programme on Friday shows a discussion between young people, teachers and parents. (Film interview with two teenagers.)

Average time per week teenagers spend on different activities: 13 to 16-year-olds.

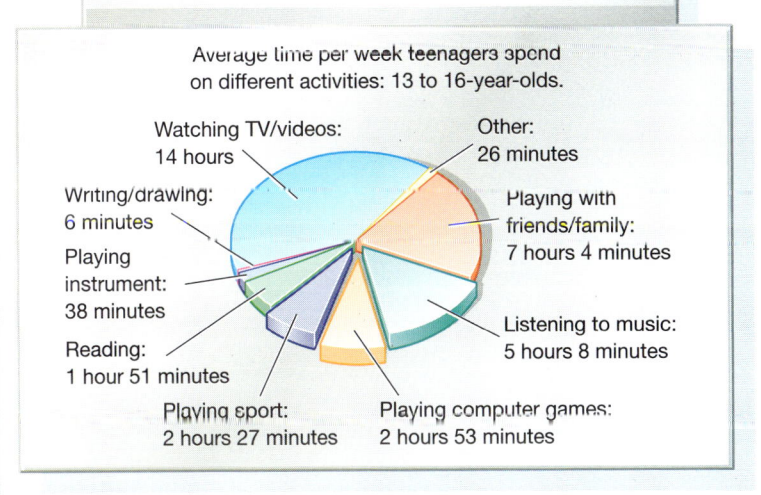

- Watching TV/videos: 14 hours
- Other: 26 minutes
- Writing/drawing: 6 minutes
- Playing with friends/family: 7 hours 4 minutes
- Playing instrument: 38 minutes
- Listening to music: 5 hours 8 minutes
- Reading: 1 hour 51 minutes
- Playing sport: 2 hours 27 minutes
- Playing computer games: 2 hours 53 minutes

Unit 9 The news

Evaluation: Listening

1 Looking at listening

1.1 Listening and you

Work by yourself. Answer the questions in the questionnaire. Compare your answers with other students.

1.2 Listening in the classroom

Look back at the listening you did in Theme C. What problems did you have?
Was it difficult or easy to listen? Did you enjoy it? Why/why not? How can you improve your listening ability?

Write about your ideas and give your paper to your teacher. (You don't have to put your name on it.)

1.3 Be independent!
Improve your listening!

Work in pairs or a small group. Brainstorm some ways you can develop your listening.

What can you listen to? For example: short stories, songs, the radio …
What can you do to improve your listening? For example: play a cassette and try to repeat it, play a cassette and write down the words …

Tell your teacher your ideas. Agree when and how you can get more listening practice, in class or at home.

Questionnaire
Listening

1 Do you enjoy listening work in class?
- ☐ a Yes, a lot.
- ☐ b Sometimes.
- ☐ c Not very much.
- ☐ d No, almost never.

2 What makes listening work difficult?
- ☐ a It is difficult to hear the cassette.
- ☐ b It is too fast.
- ☐ c I need to hear it more than once.
- ☐ d I don't understand the accents.
- ☐ e I don't understand the topic.
- Other reason:

3 While you are listening, do you
- ☐ a listen for every word?
- ☐ b predict what most of the sentence will be?
- ☐ c find it hard to concentrate all the time?
- ☐ d aim to understand the main idea?

4 When you finish listening to the cassette,
- ☐ a can you remember exact phrases?
- ☐ b can you remember the main idea?
- ☐ c can you tell someone what the text was about?
- ☐ d do you worry if you don't hear / understand everything?

Theme D
Spinning in space

1 Communication technology

1.1 Spreading the news

How many ways can you think of to get news to other places? Work in a small group and brainstorm your ideas.

newspapers — film — GETTING THE NEWS — letters

Share your ideas with the rest of the class.

1.2 The words you know

What words do you know that connect with each idea from Exercise 1.1? Make a word map around your ideas.

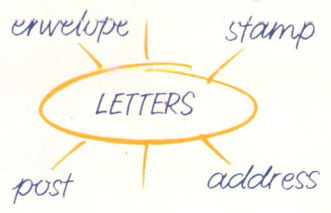

envelope — stamp — LETTERS — post — address

2 Take a look at Theme D

Look at the pictures. Where can you find them in Units 10-12 and Option D?
Read the contents page. In which unit or units can you:

- learn about modern communication technology?
- find out about Samantha's problem?
- read about a natural satellite?
- learn some grammar?
- try to influence the future?

Around the Theme

UNIT

10 TOPIC AND LANGUAGE
Messages through space
page 42

How do pictures travel to our television screens? How can we talk to people on the other side of the world on the telephone? Find out about what satellites do and learn about the passive voice.

11 OUT AND ABOUT
Too afraid to speak
page 46

Samantha sees a boy from school doing something suspicious in the shopping centre. Who should she tell? What do you think?

12 REVISION
page 48

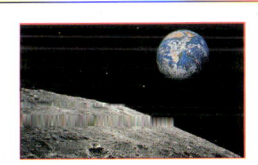

Revise the vocabulary and the passive form, present perfect, past simple and future in Unit 12 and read about the natural satellite – the moon.

OPTION D FLUENCY
A letter for the world
page 83

World decision makers

Who decides our future? What hopes do you have for the future? Write a letter to the important decision-makers of our time.

Media;
communications;
curriculum links
with Physics;
Present passive

1 *Reading and discussion*

2 *Reading and vocabulary*
WB Ex. 1

10 Messages through space
Topic and language

1 The popularity of television

In Britain more than 95% of homes have a TV. Children aged between 11 and 16 watch an average of three hours of TV a day. Is it the same in your country?

Work alone and answer the questionnaire.

Compare your answers with other students in your class.

Questionnaire

1. Is there a TV in your home? Yes/No
2. How many TVs are there in your home? 
3. Are they colour or black and white?
4. Do you have a TV in your bedroom? Yes/No
5. Do you watch TV every day? Yes/No 
6. How many hours of TV do you watch every week?
7. What are your favourite programmes?
8. What's your favourite TV channel?
9. Do you have satellite TV? Yes/No
10. How many satellite channels are there in your country? Where do they come from?

2 Satellites in the sky

2.1 What don't you know?

Have you ever seen a satellite in the sky? Tell the class what you saw.

What do you know about satellites? What don't you know? Work with a partner and make a list.

Satellites
Things I know   Things I don't know
They send   How big are
TV pictures.   satellites?

Compare your lists with the rest of the class.

2.2 Guess!

Here are some facts and figures about satellites. What do you think they mean?

1. 300,000 kilometres per second
   the speed radio and television signals travel
2. 35,880 kilometres over the equator
3. 11,000 kilometres an hour
4. 10–12 years

2.3 Find some answers

Now read about satellites and check your answers to Exercise 2.2.

How many questions from Exercise 2.1 can you answer now?

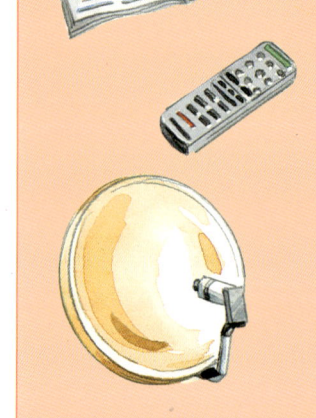

42 Messages through space

Satellites

Satellites in our lives

Satellites are an important part of our ordinary lives. For example, the information for weather forecasts is sent by satellite. Some satellites have cameras which take photographs of the Earth to show how clouds are moving. Satellites are also used to connect our international phone calls.

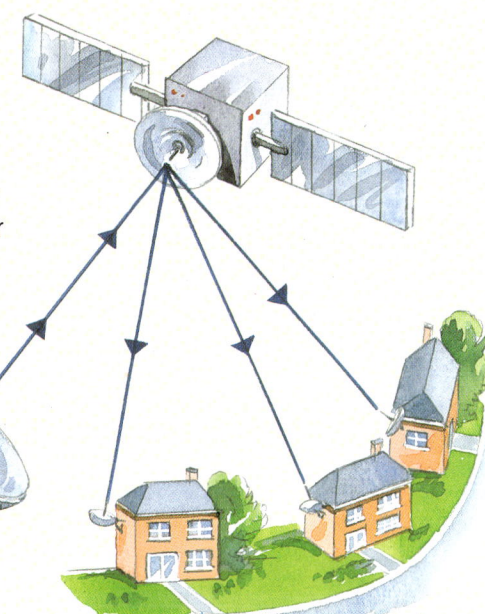

Computer connections of the World Wide Web and Internet also use satellites. Many of our TV programmes come to us through satellites. Aeroplane pilots also sometimes use a satellite to help them find their exact location.

An astronaut repairs a satellite

Television satellites

We use satellites to send television pictures from one part of the world to another. They are usually 35,880 kilometres above the equator. Sometimes we can see a satellite in the sky and it seems to stay in the same place. This is because it is moving around the world at 11,000 kilometres an hour – exactly the same speed that the Earth rotates. A satellite must orbit the Earth with its antennae facing the Earth. Sometimes, it moves away from its orbit, so there are little rockets on it which are used to put the satellite back in the right position. This usually happens about every five or six days.

The Earth's biggest dustbin?

Space is not empty! Every week, more and more satellites are sent into space to orbit the Earth. A satellite usually works for about 10–12 years. Satellites which are broken are sometimes repaired by astronauts or sometimes they are brought back to Earth to be repaired. Often, very old or broken satellites are left in space to orbit the Earth for a very long time. This is very serious because some satellites use nuclear power and they can crash into each other.

2.4 New words

Here are some words from the texts. Can you put them into pairs with similar meanings?

(power) orbit position move around send (energy) place about transmit approximately

Now put one of the words into each sentence.

1 Every day, more satellites .... the Earth.
2 TV stations .... signals to the satellites.
3 .... 200 million people watched the Olympic Games at the same time on television.
4 Each satellite has a different .... in space.
5 Satellites use batteries and solar ....

Unit 10 Topic and language   43

3 *Present passive*
WB Ex. 2; TB Ws. 10

4 *Language Record*

3 Language focus The passive

3.1 Active or passive?

Look at these sentences. What differences can you see between the sentences in List A and the sentences in List B? Tell the class your ideas.

> List A
> They send more satellites into space every year.
> We use satellites in many different ways.
> Television companies use satellites to broadcast television signals.
> We often make telephone calls via satellites.
> Pilots sometimes need satellites for navigation.

> List B
> Every year more satellites are sent into space.
> Satellites are used in many different ways.
> Satellites are used to broadcast television signals.
> Telephone calls are often made via satellites.
> Sometimes, satellites are needed for navigation.

How do you say the sentences in List B in your language?

3.2 When do we use the passive?

The sentences in List B are examples of the passive voice. The passive is often used in English when:

a the action is more important than who does it.

> Millions of letters are posted every day.

b you describe a process.

> Signals are transmitted to a satellite. They are then sent to another country.

c you write a rule.

> Ball games are not allowed here.

Read these passive sentences. Write a, b, or c next to each one.

1 The TV cameras are put into position.
2 Coffee and orange juice are provided for the news team.
3 The studio staff are asked to be quiet.
4 The director says, 'No visitors are allowed now!'
5 In the TV studio, pictures and sound are recorded on the camera. They are then sent across the world.

3.3 How to form the passive

Look at the passive sentences in Exercises 4.1 and 4.2. You can find the same verb in every passive sentence. What is it?

> Subject + ? + past participle

Look at the sentences again. Why is the verb sometimes singular and sometimes plural?

Look at the irregular verb list on page 90.

44 Messages through space

3.4 PRACTICE In the campsite

Write the correct form of the verb 'be' in the gaps.

INFORMATION

1 The campsite gates ..... opened at 7.00 am. They .... closed at 11.45 pm.
2 On the last day, guests ..... asked to leave before 10.00 am.
3 No foreign money ..... accepted.
4 The swimming pool .... cleaned between 7.00 am and 8.00 am. Please do not use it then.
5 Children under 12 years ..... not allowed in the swimming pool without an adult.
6 Dogs ..... not allowed in the campsite.
7 Fresh milk ..... sold in the campsite shop every morning.

3.5 Letters around the world

Read about how letters are delivered. Use the passive to describe the sequence.

1 Letters .... (collect) from the post box. They .... (take) to the main post office.

2 A machine .... (use) to separate the letters into 'first class' and 'second class'.

3 The letters .... (send) to the coding machine. Here the postcode .... (type) into a computer. Small blue dots .... (print) on each envelope.

4 The letters for different countries .... (put) into different post bags.

5 The bags .... (transport) by land, sea and air.

6 The letters .... (deliver) a few days later!

4 Your Language Record

4.1 Your Grammar Record

Make notes about the Present passive in your *Grammar Record*. Make notes about how to form sentences in the Present passive. Look at Exercise 4 and the Language summaries in your Workbook for ideas.

4.2 Your Record of Language Use

Look back at Unit 10. Are there more words and phrases you can add to your *Record of Language Use*? Check your record with this list:

Nouns average satellite weather forecast World Wide Web location dustbin antennae postcode envelope

Verbs orbit crash rotate provide allow transport deliver

Adjectives ordinary exact broken

Time to spare?

Choose one of these exercises.

1 Look at the *Help yourself list* on pages 91–2. Make an exercise about this Unit.

2 What rules do you have at home or at school? Look at Exercise 4.4. Write a list of new or old rules for your home or school using the Present passive.

3 Write about your favourite TV programme. What is it about? What has happened in it?

Unit 10 Topic and language 45

Discussion about the right thing to do; talking about past events
WB Optional Unit D Ways to reading (2)

1. *Discussion*
2. *Listening*
3. *Language focus*
4. *Decide …*

11 Too afraid to speak
Out and about with English

1 What do you think?

Discuss these questions with the class:

What kinds of bad things do you see other students doing sometimes?
If you see a student doing something suspicious outside school, who do you think you should tell?
Do you think you should 'tell tales' about other students?
Is it easy to tell parents and teachers about other students' bad behaviour?

2 What happened?

2.1 A local news story

Samantha and Rebecca are doing their homework. Look at the picture in Exercise 1. What do you think Samantha is telling Rebecca?

🔊 Listen to Part A. The television is on. What news story do they hear? Why do you think Samantha is worried? Share your ideas with the class.

2.2 What should she do?

🔊 Listen to Part B. Why is Samantha worried? What do you think she should do now? What would you do?

Have you ever been in a situation like this? Do you think it is more important to report a crime or to protect yourself?

3 Inside the text
Question tags

Look back through the dialogue in Part A. What is the question tag which follows 'Let's'? Find two examples. Make up two more of your own. Add them to your *Record of Language Use*.

How many other examples of question tags can you find? Add them to your *Record of Language Use*.

4 Decide …

Work by yourself or in a small group. Choose **a**, **b** or **c**.

a A letter

Imagine you are Samantha. Write a letter to a friend describing what happened in the shopping centre.

b Samantha tells someone

Samantha decides to tell someone – her parents, the head teacher or the police. You decide. In pairs or in small groups prepare the dialogue. When you are ready, act it out for the class or record it on a cassette.

c You decide!

Look at page 91–2 for ideas. You could …
– write an article for the local paper describing what happened.
– work in pairs. One of you interviews the shop assistant from Sound Store who describes what happened in the shop.
– have a discussion in your group and decide what should happen to Jack Brinsdon.

Samantha sees a crime

Part A

SAMANTHA: We've got loads of homework tonight, haven't we?
REBECCA: Yes, three subjects! Maths …
SAMANTHA: Yes, and I don't understand it, do you?
REBECCA: No! It's really difficult.
SAMANTHA: OK. Let's start with Maths, shall we?

TV NEWS: And now for the local news …
SAMANTHA: We're on page 45, aren't we?
REBECCA: Yes, Exercise 4.
TV NEWS: Police are looking for a young man …
REBECCA: I don't understand this, do you?
SAMANTHA: No, not very well.
TV NEWS: … the young man who was in Millbroad Shopping Centre this afternoon is white …
SAMANTHA: Let's read it together, shall we?
REBECCA: OK.
TV NEWS: … and aged about 15. At 4.30 this afternoon …
REBECCA: What does this mean, Samantha?
SAMANTHA: Sshhh!!
TV NEWS: …who took four CDs and ten cassettes from Sound Store in the shopping centre this afternoon. Anyone who saw this incident should telephone …

Part B

SAMANTHA: I saw a boy running away from Sound Store this afternoon!
REBECCA: Did he see you?
SAMANTHA: Yes, he knocked into me.
TV NEWS: *… the video cameras in the shopping centre recorded some pictures of the boy talking to a young girl.*
REBECCA: You didn't talk to him, did you?
SAMANTHA: No … yes … er, no. He told me not to tell anyone.
REBECCA: Tell anyone what? Did he have the CDs and cassettes?
SAMANTHA: I don't know … probably …
REBECCA: Well, who was it?
SAMANTHA: You know, Jack Brinsdon.
REBECCA: I know him … a horrible boy … always in trouble.
SAMANTHA: Yes, for stealing and fighting.
REBECCA: I think you should tell the police or someone, Samantha, don't you?
TV NEWS: *… the boy might have a knife. The police would like to find him as soon as possible.*
SAMANTHA: I'm frightened! He will know it's me if I tell someone.
FATHER: What's the matter, Samantha?

Idiom box

Knock into someone accidentally pushing into someone when you're in a hurry
(to be) in trouble to have some problems
What's the matter? What's the problem? What's wrong with you?

Unit 11 Out and about with English

Revision of Units 4–11

1. *Self assessment*
2. *Vocabulary*
3. *'will', 'going to', Future perfect*
4. *Present perfect*
5. *Question tags*

12 Revision

1 How well do you know it?

How well do you think you know the English you learnt in Themes B and C? Put a tick (√) in the table

	very well	OK	a little
New vocabulary. (Theme B)			
Future (will, going to, future perfect)			
Present perfect			
Question tags			
New vocabulary (Theme C)			

2 The words you met

Can you write the correct words in the puzzle? You can find them all in Unit 4, Exercise 7.

What word does the puzzle spell?

1. If a lot of people like something, then it is p............ (adjective)
2. Without this, we can't think! (noun)
3. All solid objects have height, width and .... (noun)
4. A person who can't see is .... (adjective)
5. Illness (noun)
6. Precisely (adverb)
7. Not enough of something (noun)
8. Stop work to get better pay, etc.: go on .... (noun)
9. Join (verb)
10. The place where you are going (noun)
11. The reason why something happens (noun)

3 Talking about the future

3.1 'Going to or will?'

Are these sentences about predictions, plans or things certain to happen? Complete each sentence with 'be going to' or 'will'.

1. Do you think it .... rain next week?
2. I .... buy a new bag tomorrow. I've lost my old one.
3. In the future, many people .... work at home.
4. Next summer, I .... learn to play tennis.
5. Who .... win the next World Cup in football, do you think?
6. John .... paint his bedroom tomorrow. He's already bought the paint.

3.2 Answer the questions

Can you answer these questions?

By the end of this year …

1. how long will you have studied English?
   I will have studied English for .... years.
2. how many lessons of English will you have had?
3. how many units of this book will you have completed, do you think?
4. how many different English teachers will have taught you?
5. how many different course books will you have used?

48 Revision

4 Experiences

You can use the Present perfect to ask a question about experiences:

Have you ever been on a motor-cycle?

and the Past simple to answer it.

Yes, I have. I went on one last summer.

Work with your partner again and ask each other some questions. Answer:

No, I haven't. *or* Yes, I have. I …

Have you ever watched TV at 3 o'clock in the morning?
Have you ever visited a television station?
Have you ever been to an English-speaking country?
Have you ever skied?
Have you ever talked to an English or an American person?
Have you ever eaten raw fish?
Have you ever been on a ship?
Have you ever …

5 What shall we watch?

5.1 The week on TV

Joe and Martha are talking about the TV programmes they are going to watch in the next few days. Choose the correct question tags from the box.

| aren't we? | don't you? | have you? | haven't we? | is it? |
| isn't it? | isn't it? | shall we? | shall we? |

JOE: Look, Martha. Look what's on on Saturday. That's the programme you like about animals, ¹................? It's before dinner. Let's watch that together, ²................?

MARTHA: OK. You want to watch that space film at 7 o'clock, ³................?

JOE: No, we can't. We're going to Grandma's after dinner on Saturday, ⁴................?

MARTHA: Oh, yes, that's right.

JOE: Let's look at Sunday. You haven't seen the new children's spy story yet, ⁵................?

MARTHA: No, I haven't. We'll watch that then at 7.30.

JOE: Now, Monday, there's my sports programme. Great! Let's watch this film at 6.30, ⁶................? It looks interesting.

MARTHA: What's it about?

JOE: Um … it says 'an exciting adventure in 19th-century France'.

MARTHA: It's not called 'Freedom for a rose', ⁷................?

JOE: Yes, it is. Why?

MARTHA: We've seen it already, ⁸................?

JOE: Oh, yes. I remember. It's very boring, ⁹................?

5.2 What can you say?

What can you say in each of these situations?
Write a sentence for each one and use question tags.

1 You think the bus leaves at 10 am.
   The bus leaves at 10 am, doesn't it?
2 You think the new Mash Boys song is terrible.
3 You think the History homework was on page 45.
4 You think your friend's new phone number is 070 1070.
5 You think the new Maths teacher is very nice.
6 You think you have already seen the new film at the cinema.
7 You think you have to do the English homework for tomorrow.

6 *Vocabulary*
7 *Present passive*

6 The words you met

6.1 Verb, noun or both?

Here are some of the words you saw in Units 8–11. Some words are nouns, some are verbs and some are both. Write them in the right place in the diagram.

satellite   weather forecast   signal   location
dustbin   antennae   transmit   orbit   crash
rotate   provide   allow   transport   deliver

Compare circles with other students in your class.

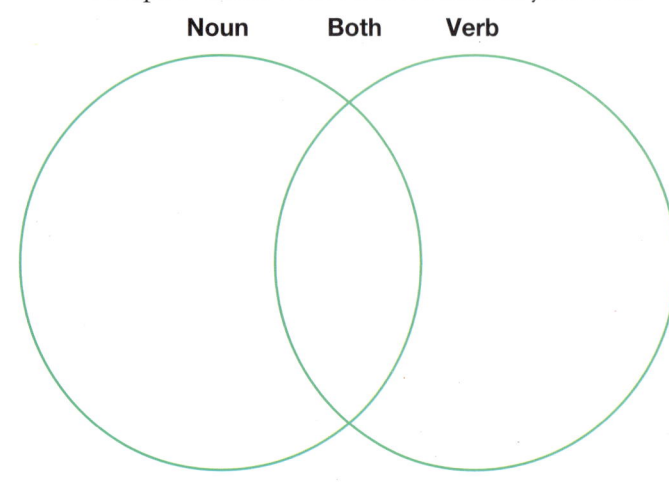

Noun   Both   Verb

6.2 The moon: a natural satellite

Read about the moon. Choose a word from Exercise 6.1 to complete the sentences. Put the word in the correct form.

Look back at the text. Write N (noun) or V (verb) over each word that you wrote in the gaps.

6.3 Word pairs: adjective and noun

Choose the noun which we use most often with the adjective.

1 tragic   a broadcast   b advertisement
   c producer   d accident
2 balanced   a gossip   b report   c politician
   d crime
3 ordinary   a dinosaur   b smoke   c people
   d president
4 foreign   a altitude   b home   c news
   d coincidence
5 surprising   a channel   b economics
   c coincidence   d antennae

Write the correct word pair in these sentences.

1 Many people are more interested in home news than in ....
2 When twins meet after many years there are often many .... in their lives.
3 The young journalist was killed in a .... in Albania.
4 The BBC tries to present .... on the news.
5 Human interest stories are often about ....

A natural satellite

The moon is a natural satellite which ..... around the Earth. Normally, we only see one side of the moon because the moon ..... at the same speed as the Earth. In 1969, the Apollo XI rocket went to the moon. It ..... pictures of the moon back to Earth. From the pictures we could see that the moon has deep valleys. These valleys were made when meteors ..... into the moon.

The climate on the moon is terrible. There isn't any air on the moon, so the difference between daytime and night-time temperatures is enormous. An imaginary .... for the moon would say, 'The temperature today will be 130 degrees centigrade. At night, it will drop to minus 173 degrees centigrade!' The average difference in day and night temperatures on the moon is 300 degrees centigrade.

7 How do they do that?

7.1 Making paper

Can you match the two parts of the sentence to explain how paper is made?

1 The trees
2 The logs
3 Each log
4 The small pieces of wood
5 Alkali
6 This mixture
7 Water and dye
8 The paper mixture (pulp)

a is cut into very small pieces.
b are taken to paper mills.
c are mixed with acid.
d are cut into logs.
e is then heated.
f are added.
g is added.
h is pressed between rollers to remove the water.

7.2 Making glass bottles

Look at the pictures which show how we make glass bottles. Use the Present passive to describe the sequence.

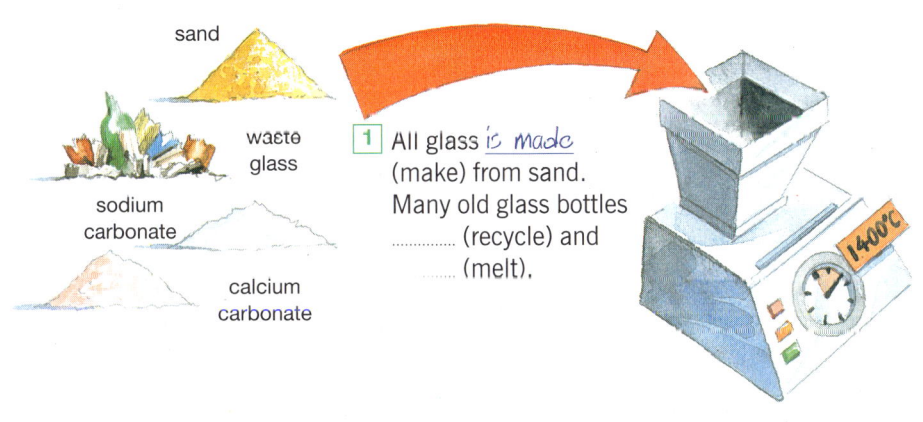

1 All glass *is made* (make) from sand. Many old glass bottles .... (recycle) and .... (melt).

2 Sodium carbonate .... (add) to reduce the melting point of the sand. Calcium carbonate .... (mix) with the other raw materials to make the glass waterproof. The sand, old bottles and the chemicals .... (put) into the furnace.
The furnace .... (heat) to 1,400 degrees centigrade so that the sand melts.

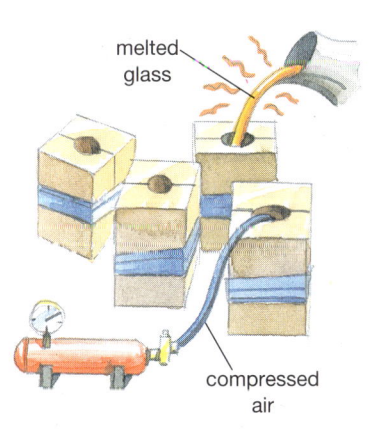

3 A small amount of melted glass .... (drop) into the mould. Air .... (force) into the mould to shape the glass.

4 The finished bottles .... (take out) of the mould.

Unit 12 Revision 51

Evaluation: Reading

1 Looking at reading

1.1 Reading and you

Answer the questions in the questionnaire. Compare your answers with other students in your class.

1.2 Reading in the classroom

Look back at the reading you did in Theme D. What problems did you have? Was it difficult or easy to read? Did you enjoy it? How can you improve your reading next time?

Write about your ideas and give your paper to your teacher. (You don't have to put your name on it.)

1.3 Be independent!
Improve your reading!

Work in pairs or a small group. Brainstorm some ways you can get extra reading practice.

What can you read? For example: newspapers, magazines, poems ...
What can you read about? For example: sport, music ...
How can you check your reading? For example: make your own exercises, make wordlists ...
How can you have more fun reading? For example: start a reading group, make a book review poster ...

Tell your teacher your ideas. Agree when you can do it, in class or at home.

Questionnaire
Reading

1 Do you like reading in English?
- a Yes, a lot.
- b It's OK.
- c No, I don't like it.
  Why?

2 When you read something in English, do you:
- a read the titles first and think about them?
- b look at the pictures first?
- c read every word?
- d read the first sentence of each paragraph and then read the whole text?
- e do something else?

3 While you are reading in English, do you:
- a look up all the new words in a dictionary immediately?
- b write down all the new words and look them up later?
- c guess some of them and write down the others?
- d ignore the words you don't understand?
- e do something else?

4 When you have finished reading something in English, do you:
- a write down all the new words in a Vocabulary Record?
- b read it again to check your understanding?
- c ask yourself questions about the text?
- d read it again as fast as you can just for fun?
- e do something else?

Theme E
Wonders of the world

1 World Heritage sites

Look at the world map on pages 88–9. Are there any World Heritage sites in or near your country? Look through the list of places. Do you know about any of them? What places in your country do you think should be World Heritage sites?

2 Take a look at Theme E

Look at the pictures. Where can you find them in Units 13-15 and Option E?
Look at the descriptions of each Unit. In which unit or units can you:

– learn about the work of an international organisation?
– learn some grammar?
– read about the damage that vandals can do?
– read about mysterious places?
– learn about strange and wonderful natural phenomena?
– discuss whether you think Samantha is right?

Around the Theme

UNIT

13 TOPIC AND LANGUAGE
Our heritage
page 54

Learn about the work of the World Heritage organisation and how it helps to preserve our history. Read about the problems of vandalism at some important sites. Learn how to make conditional sentences in English.

14 TOPIC AND LANGUAGE
Natural wonders
page 58

Nature is amazing! Learn about some incredible natural heritage sites - from spectacular water falls in Africa to the strange stones in Ireland. Learn how to use the passive to talk about how things were done.

15 ALL ABOUT...
Mysteries of the past
page 62

Who made it? Why did they make it? Where did they come from? Read about the mysteries of places in Africa, and South and North America.

OPTION E OUT AND ABOUT
A sponsored fast
page 84

Samantha is asking for money. Would you give it to her? Do you think she has a good reason to ask for it?

Places of historical importance; curriculum links with History and Geography; second conditional

1 *Discussion, reading*

2 *Listening*

3 *Discussion, reading*
IT A and B

Inside the text
A *Comprehension*
B *Vocabulary*

13 Our heritage
Topic and language

1 Some famous places

1.1 Where are they?

Look at the pictures. Do you know where these places are? What are the people doing?
Have you ever been to a famous place? What did you do there? Tell the class.

1.2 Postcards from around the world

Read the postcards. Can you match them to the correct picture?

1

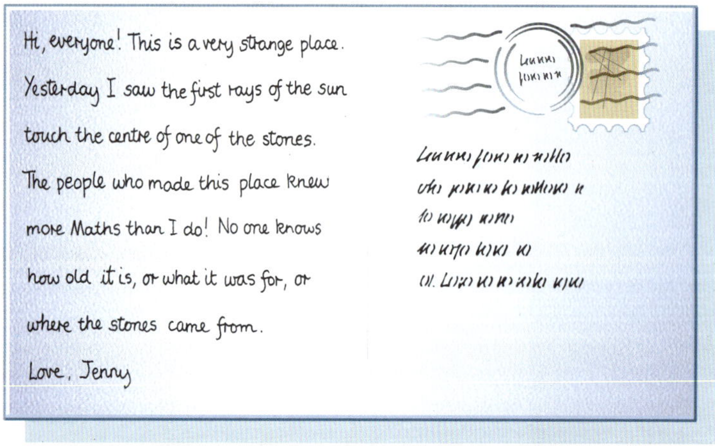

Hi, everyone! This is a very strange place. Yesterday I saw the first rays of the sun touch the centre of one of the stones. The people who made this place knew more Maths than I do! No one knows how old it is, or what it was for, or where the stones came from.
Love, Jenny

2

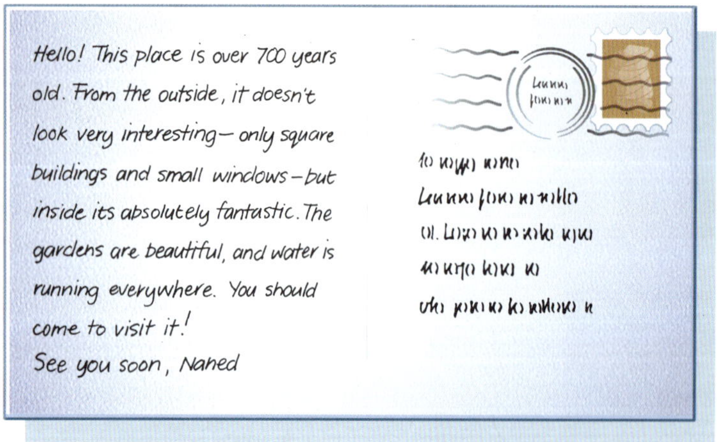

Hello! This place is over 700 years old. From the outside, it doesn't look very interesting — only square buildings and small windows — but inside its absolutely fantastic. The gardens are beautiful, and water is running everywhere. You should come to visit it!
See you soon, Nahed

2 What makes a place famous?

2.1 What do you think?

What makes a place famous? Why do you think people want to visit famous places? Work in a small group and brainstorm your ideas.

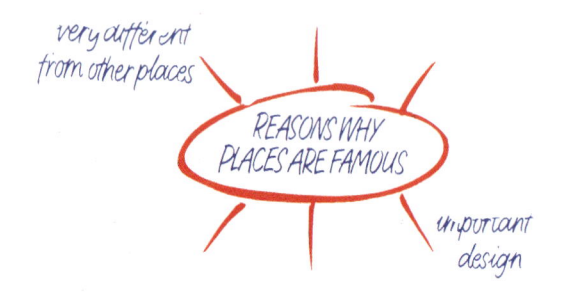

very different from other places
REASONS WHY PLACES ARE FAMOUS
important design

2.2 Our heritage

Jean Duclos works for The World Heritage Organisation — an organisation which looks after famous places in the world. Listen. Can you add some more reasons to your ideas map?

3 Saving our past for our future

3.1 Looking after the past

Do you think it is important to look after historic places? What do you think is the biggest problem for old places?

3.2 How can we look after the past?

Read the text. Which of these ideas does the text mention?

building high fences   installing TV cameras
using guard dogs   paying entrance fees
reducing pollution   removing the valuable items
closing the sites   educating people about history

HOW CAN WE LOOK AFTER THE PAST?

Our children and grandchildren may not have a chance to visit many of the most famous places around the world. War, weather, age, traffic and pollution damage these famous places. There is a need for constant renovation. But looking after these places often costs more than one country can afford.

The World Heritage Organisation

In the early 1970s, world governments decided that if they joined together, they would be able to preserve our history. If every country paid some money, they said, it would be possible to look after important historic places. Also, if they discovered that a monument needed urgent help, they would have money for repairs. For these reasons, countries around the world united to form The World Heritage Organisation in 1972. Today, the organisation helps to maintain and restore the most important places from our history.

Vandalism: one of the biggest problems

However, one of the biggest problems for historic places is vandalism. People sometimes enter the sites and destroy or damage the buildings. At some sites, such as Stonehenge in England, governments have built high fences to protect the site from vandals.

There are many different ideas about how to solve the problem of vandalism. Some experts say that if guards patrolled the sites, vandals would not be able to get in. Other experts say that if they installed more television cameras, they would not need so many security guards. At other sites, there are not enough guides, and visitors can walk around alone. If every site had more guides it would be easier to look after these famous places.

Other experts say that the best solution is education. If people learned to respect history, they would not destroy or damage it. They would also want to spend money to look after old places. For this reason, The World Heritage Organisation helps to spread information about the value of historic sites.

Stonehenge, Wiltshire, England

The Taj Mahal, Agra, India

El Alhambra, Granada, Spain

The Great Wall of China

Inside the text

A Where do they go?

Where can you put these sentences into the text? Compare your ideas with your neighbour.

1. However, high fences are very ugly and very unfriendly.
2. This makes it very easy for vandals to cause damage when no one is looking.
3. The problem is that all these solutions are very expensive.
4. They sometimes spray paint on the walls of buildings or steal valuable items like mosaics.

B Different words, similar meanings

Find words in the text which have a similar meaning to these words:

1. places: s.....................
2. destroy: d.....................
3. protect: p....................., m.....................
4. united: j..................... t.....................
5. repair: r.....................
6. enter: g..................... i.....................

Choose five words and write a sentence with each word. Leave a gap for the word. Give the sentences to your partner to complete.

Unit 13 Topic and language 55

[4] *Listening*
[5] *Second conditional* WB Ex. 2
[6] *Language Record*

[4] A talking monument

Look at the pictures on page 55. Listen. One of the monuments is talking about the problems it has had. Which monument is it?

Listen again. Which of these problems does it mention?

traffic fumes	wars
graffiti	earthquakes and volcanoes
floods	heavy lorries and coaches
snow and ice	people's feet

[5] Language focus
Second conditional

5.1 What do you say?

How do you say these sentences in your language?

If guards patrolled the sites, vandals would not be able to get in.
If people learned to respect history, they would not destroy it.

Look back at the text in Exercise 3. Find some more examples of sentences with 'would'. What is the form of the verb after 'if'? What is the form of the verb after 'would'?

5.2 What does it mean?

Sentences like the ones in Exercise 5.1 are examples of the second conditional. You can use the second conditional if you want to talk about things that are not real now. They can be very improbable:

If it rained every day, we would live in boats.

or a little bit improbable:

If I met the American President, I would invite him to my house.

or possible:

If I knew the answer, I would tell you.

You can also use it to make suggestions:

If I were you, I would go to bed.

5.3 Make a sentence

Can you match the two parts of each sentence?

1 If more people knew about the sites …   a … I would travel round the world.
2 If we had a lot of money …   b … there would be even more visitors.
3 If I had a lot of time …   c … we could repair a lot more sites.
4 If I were you …   d … some children would be happy.
5 If the government closed all the schools …   e … I would go to a dentist with that toothache.

Which sentences are suggestions? Which sentences are very improbable? Which are probable and which are possible?

5.4 How to form the second conditional

How can you describe the second conditional?

If it rained every day we would live in boats.
If + …

Test yourself! Fill in the correct form of the verb in brackets. Add 'would' and other words where necessary.

1 What *would you* do if you *saw* a ghost? (do, see)
2 If you .... banana skins, you .... very sick. (eat, be)
3 Where .... for your holiday if you .... a million dollars? (go, win)
4 Who .... for help if you .... it? (ask, need)
5 When .... to bed if you could go when you liked? (go)

Be careful! The verb after 'if' has the same form as the past tense, but the meaning is present or future.

56 Our heritage

5.5 What would happen if … ?

What would happen if the world was a very different place?

What would happen if trees could walk?

If trees could walk, we would have high walls around our gardens.

… they would go to warm countries in the winter.

Choose some of the questions below. Write about them.

- What would happen if Martians landed on Earth? 
- What would happen if you were the head teacher of your school? 
- What would happen if it didn't rain again? 
- What would happen if there was another ice age? 
- What would happen if the seas all dried up? 
- What would happen if no one needed to sleep? 
- What would happen if the Earth stopped turning?

6 Your Language Record

6.1 Your Grammar Record

Make notes about the second conditional in your *Grammar Record*. Make notes about how to form it and how to use it. Look at Exercise 4 and the Language summaries in your Workbook for ideas.

6.2 Your Record of Language Use

Look at Unit 13. Are there more words and phrases you can add to your *Record of Language Use*? Check your record with this list.

Verbs touch damage afford join together preserve unite maintain restore repair destroy protect patrol install respect

Nouns ray monument chance renovation vandal vandalism fence guard guide

Adjectives interesting constant urgent

Work alone. Choose six or more words. Write a word puzzle – a word search or a crossword – or look through the Student's Book or Workbook for ideas. Write and/or draw some clues. Give your puzzle to your partner.

Time to spare?

Choose one of these exercises.

1. Look at the *Help yourself list* on pages 91–2. Make an exercise about this Unit.

2. Think of a famous place in your country that you know. Write a postcard from there.

3. Think of a problem in your town or school, for example, parking, traffic, litter. How can you solve the problem? Write as many suggestions as you can using the second conditional.

Unit 13 Topic and language

Natural sites; curriculum links with Geography, Science and History; 'unless' and Past passive

1 *Discussion*

2 *Listening; 'unless'*
WB Ex. 2

3 *Reading*
WB Ex. 1

14 Natural wonders
Topic and language

1 Nature around you

Are there any national parks or conservation areas near where you live? Why are they special? Have you visited them? What can you see and do there? Tell the class your ideas.

2 Caring for nature

2.1 What do you think?

Do you think we should protect some natural places? Which type of places? Why?

2.2 Special places

🔊 Listen to Kate Lander talking to Jean Duclos about reasons for protecting nature. How many of these reasons does he mention?

- the home of wild animals
- an isolated place
- the home of rare plants
- a beautiful view
- very large places
- an unusual place
- the home of endangered species
- the home of a certain group of people

Look at the pictures on these pages. Which reasons would he give for protecting each place, do you think? Share your ideas with the class.

▲ Serengeti National Park, Tanzania

2.3 Listen again, listen carefully

🔊 Listen again. What explanations does Jean Duclos give for protecting nature? Can you complete these sentences?

Unless we protect nature, …
Unless we protect the home of those animals, …
Unless we protect beautiful places, …
Unless we protect some plants, …

▼ Victoria Falls, on the border of Zambia and Zimbabwe

▼ Tongariro Volcano, New Zealand

Galapagos Islands, Pacific Ocean

The Galapagos Islands are 1,100 kilometres west of Ecuador in South America. There are many species of reptiles, birds and plants which are only found here. These animals survived on the islands because they were isolated from dangerous animals, disease and people.

The islands are particularly famous for the huge tortoises. They are so heavy that you need six or eight people to lift them. They can live for about 100 years and can weigh about 270 kilos. The islands were once visited many times by sailors, explorers, hunters and fishermen who killed the slow, friendly animals for their meat. Some tortoises were taken off the islands for zoos or private collections. Some were also killed in forest fires in 1994. The tortoises are now an endangered species. There are now only about 6,000 left. Now, they and their home are protected.

The Galapagos Islands, Ecuador

The Giant's Causeway, Northern Ireland

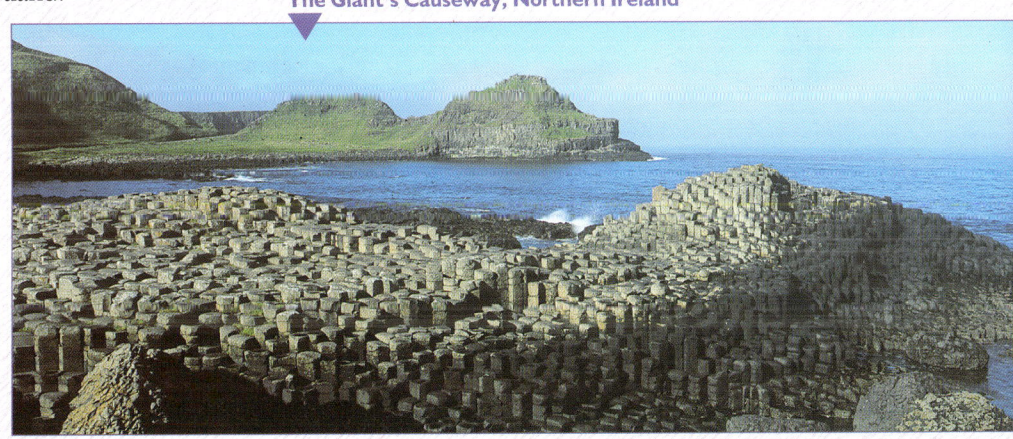

The Giant's Causeway is one of the strangest rock formations in the world. There are many myths and legends about this strange place. Local people say that the causeway was built by an enormous giant, Finn MacCool. They say he built it so that his giantess girlfriend could walk to him across the sea without getting wet. Other people say that the steps were put here so Irish people could walk over the sea to Scotland.

Geologists tell a different story. They say that the causeway was made about 60 million years ago from lava. The lava was thrown out of nearby volcanoes. The columns of the causeway all have a very similar pattern. Most of them are about 45 centimetres wide and many of them have six sides. Why do the columns look like that? Geologists say that after the lava cooled, it was shaped by the sea and glaciers. These constant, slow movements created the geometric design of the causeway. Every minute of every day the process continues – the Atlantic Ocean still shapes the columns today.

3 Two unique places

3.1 What do you think?

Look at the picture of the Giant's Causeway. What do you think it is? Is it natural or a man-made place, do you think?

Look at the picture of the tortoise in the Galapagos Islands. Why do you think the islands are important?

What do you think might happen if these places are not protected? Share your ideas with the class.

3.2 Read about each place

Work with a partner. One of you read about the Giant's Causeway, the other one read about the Galapagos Islands. Make notes about what you read.

The Galapagos Islands
The islands are important because:
The animals survived there because:
The tortoises are endangered because:

The Giant's Causeway
Local people say the causeway was made by:
Geologists say the causeway was made by:
The lava was shaped by:

The Giant's Causeway, Northern Ireland

Unit 14 Topic and language

4 *Past passive*
WB Ex. 3

5 *Language Record*

4 Language focus Past passive

4.1 Present passive

In Unit 10 you saw Present passive sentences like this:

> Satellites are used to broadcast television signals
> Millions of letters are posted everyday.

Can you remember how you say those sentences in your language?

How can you describe Present passive sentences?

Subject	+ ____	+ ____	
Millions of letters	are	posted	everyday.

4.2 Past passive

Can you find these sentences in the texts on page 59?

> Local people say that the causeway *was built* by an enormous giant.
> Other people say that the steps *were put* here so Irish people could walk over the sea to Scotland.
> They say that the causeway *was made* about 60 million years ago.
> The lava *was thrown* out of nearby volcanoes.

These are all examples of the Past passive. You can use the Past passive to talk about a natural or man-made place, when the *place* is more important than *who* made it, who went there, and so on.

Look at the examples again. How can you describe Past passive sentences?

Subject	+ ____	+ ____	
The steps	were	put	here so people could walk over the sea.
The causeway	was	made	about 60 million years ago.
The lava	was	thrown	out of nearby volcanoes.

Look at the text about the Galapagos Islands. How many examples of the Past passive can you find?

4.3 What do you know?

Can you join the two halves of each sentence 1–6 and a–f?

1 The new island of Surtsey, Iceland …
2 Devil's Tower, in the USA, …
3 The strange rocks in Pinnacles Desert, Australia …
4 The continents of the world …
5 The village of San Juan in Mexico …
6 Machu Picchu in Peru …

a was buried by the volcano Paricutin.
b was named after the Norse Fire Giant, Surtr.
c was discovered by Hiram Bingham in 1911.
d was used in the film *Close Encounters*.
e were made from rainwater and sand 100,000 years ago.
f were formed millions of years ago.

Write some sentences about natural and man-made places in your country. Make a 'matching halves' exercise for other students.

Surtsey Island, Iceland

Devil's Tower, USA

Pinnacles Desert, Australia

Natural wonders

4.4 The Great Rift Valley

Read about the Great Rift Valley. Write the verbs in the Past passive form.

THE GREAT RIFT VALLEY, EAST AFRICA

The Great Rift Valley runs for 4,800 kilometres from the Dead Sea to Mozambique. The views from the top of the Rift Valley are fantastic because in some places the valley is a thousand metres deep. There are many enormous lakes along the valley. The 'rift' is a piece of land like a valley which is lower than the land on each side.

The Great Rift Valley *was not made* (not make) by a river. It [1] .... (cause) by two tectonic plates in the earth which are moving apart. The land [2] .... (pull apart) by this movement which still continues today. In some places the gaps are about 60 kilometres wide. Sometimes it is difficult to see the gaps because of the lava which [3] .... (throw out) by volcanoes and then poured into the valley. When the 'Mountain of the God' volcano erupted, sodium carbonate [4] .... (blow) into the lakes. This made the water white.

Listen and check your answers.

5 Your Language Record

5.1 Your Grammar Record

Make notes about the Past passive in your *Grammar Record*. Look at Exercises 3 and 4 and the Language summaries in your Workbook for ideas.

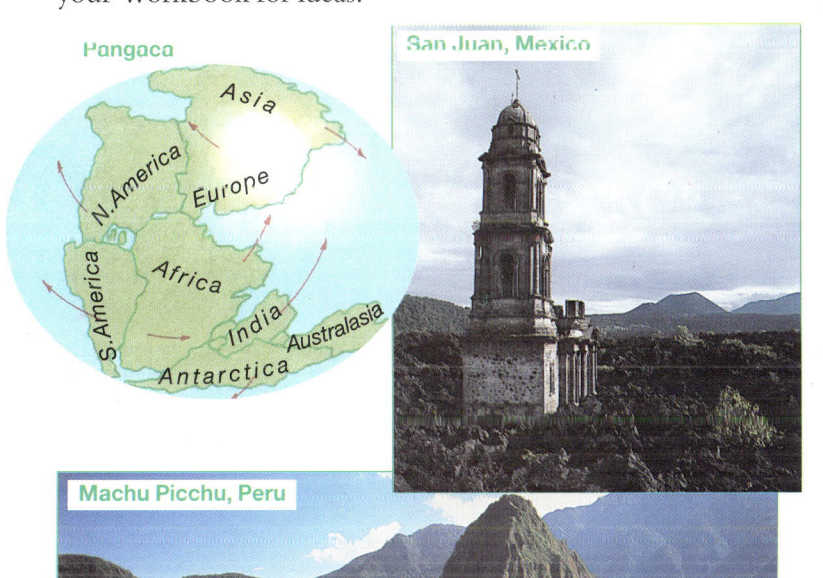

5.2 Your Record of Language Use

Look back at Unit 14. Are there more words and phrases you can add to your *Record of Language Use*? Check your record with this list:

Nouns causeway rock formation myth legend lava pattern glacier process column species collection valley

Verbs throw out cool shape create survive kill protect run move apart pull apart pour erupt

Adjectives rare endangered isolated unusual enormous similar wide constant geometric fantastic deep

Time to spare?

Choose one of these exercises.

1 Look at the *Help yourself list* on page 91–2. Make an exercise about this Unit.

2 Read the texts in Exercise 3 again. Write about a famous natural place in your country.

3 Write some 'search' questions about the places in this Unit. Give your questions to another student to answer.

Unit 14 Topic and language 61

15 ALL ABOUT...
Mysteries of the past

1 *Fluency*
2 a *Writing*
  b *You decide!*

1 All about ... the mysteries of the past!

1.1 Search!

Look at the texts on page 63. Can you find the answers to these questions?

1 Find these numbers. What do they refer to? Make notes about each one. For example:

200,000 – *the number of trees that the Anasazi people used.*

80   16   3,700   600   1150–1500
1871   25   9

2 Who built Pueblo Bonito?
3 Who is Heyerdahl? What did he think?
4 Why is the tower in Great Zimbabwe 'mysterious'?

Write some more 'search' questions for other students.

1.2 More details

Can you complete the table with information about each place?

	Pueblo Bonito	Easter Island	Great Zimbabwe
Type of building:	*large houses*	*statues*	*a small city*
Date:			
Materials used:			
Who built it?			
What is the mystery?			

Compare your table with other students in your class.

2 Decide ...

Choose a or b.

a Imagine ...

You are an explorer and you find one of the places in the pictures. Describe what you can see, what you think about it, how you found it ... use your imagination!

b You decide!

Decide what you want to do and ask your teacher. You could:

– imagine you are on Thor Heyerdahl's raft – write a diary for one day.
– write a story about another discovery.
– prepare a radio programme about mysteries of the past.
– write about a mysterious place in your country.
– write an exercise for other students.
– write a puzzle.
– make a test.
– write some questions.

Look at the *Help yourself list* on page 91–2 for ideas.

Puzzles from the Past:

Who? Why? When? How? What? Where?

Everyone likes mysteries. Nowadays scientists work with modern technology to try to find answers to the mysteries of the past. In this article we look at some of the most mysterious places in the world.

Great Zimbabwe, Zimbabwe

In 1871 Karl Mauch, a German, discovered huge stone walls in Zimbabwe, Africa. The walls covered 25 hectares around what is now called 'Great Zimbabwe'. Great Zimbabwe is the most impressive iron age site in Africa. On top of a hill, there is a large castle and underneath this is the 'Great Enclosure'. The Great Enclosure has enormous walls – sometimes 11 metres high and 1.2 metres thick. Inside the Great Enclosure there are many huts, passages and rooms and a mysterious 9-metre-high stone tower that has no stairs, no windows and no doors. Why did they build the tower? We don't know. We don't even know who built Great Zimbabwe – it is a mystery to African and foreign archaeologists. They think the Great Enclosure was built about 1,000 years ago.

Pueblo Bonito, New Mexico, USA

One thousand years ago, in the desert of the Chaco Canyon, the Anasazi people built nine multi-storey buildings called 'Great Houses'. They used stone for the walls and wood for the floors, doors and roofs. They transported more than 200,000 trees from forests almost 80 kilometres away. How did they move the trees? We don't know.

In some buildings there are huge circular rooms called 'kivas' – the biggest one is underground and it is about 16 metres wide. Why did the Anasazi build circular rooms? We don't know. Perhaps they used them for religious ceremonies or for storing crops. We know the Anasazi people abandoned the Great Houses. Why did they leave? Hunger? War? We really don't know.

Easter Island, Chile

Easter Island is in the South Pacific, 3,700 kilometres from the coast of Chile. On the island, there are 600 large statues. We don't know who built them but they were probably constructed between 1150 and 1500. We don't really know why they are there. The Norwegian explorer Thor Heyerdahl believed that they were built by people from South America. To prove this, he made a simple raft and sailed there, all the way from Peru. Archaeologists think that the statues represent dead tribal leaders. We don't know why the people who built the statues left the island. Perhaps they were killed by disease or war. Perhaps they used all the natural resources on the island. There are many unanswered questions about Easter Island.

Mysteries of the past

Evaluation: Speaking

1 Looking at speaking

1.1 Speaking and you

Work by yourself. Answer the questions in the questionnaire.

Compare your answers with other students in your class.

1.2 Speaking in the classroom

Look back at the speaking you did in Theme E. What problems did you have? Was it difficult or easy to speak in English? Did you enjoy it? Why/why not? How can you improve your speaking next time?

Write about your ideas and give your paper to your teacher. (You don't have to put your name on it.)

1.3 Be independent!
Improve your speaking!

Work in pairs or a small group. Brainstorm some ways you can get extra speaking practice.

What can you talk about? For example: films, science, travel …

How can you do it? For example: record some questions on a cassette and then try to answer them …

How can you get extra practice? For example: start an English club at school, talk to yourself in English …

Tell your teacher your ideas. Agree when you can do it, in class or at home.

Questionnaire
Speaking

1 When you have to say something in English, do you:
- ❏ a think in your language first and then translate first?
- ❏ b try to remember a complete phrase?
- ❏ c say the shortest sentence you can?
- ❏ d try to use new words you learned recently?
- ❏ e do something else?

2 While you are speaking, do you:
- ❏ a worry about your pronunciation?
- ❏ b stop to think of the correct word?
- ❏ c ask for help if you don't know the word?
- ❏ d say as little as you can?
- ❏ e say as much as you can?
- ❏ f do something else?

3 While you are speaking, do you:
- ❏ a worry about making mistakes?
- ❏ b concentrate on communicating your ideas?
- ❏ c correct your mistakes immediately?
- ❏ d think that it doesn't matter if you make a mistake?
- ❏ e do something else?

4 When you have finished speaking, do you:
- ❏ a think about what you could have said?
- ❏ b check that the other person has understood you?
- ❏ c feel embarrassed about what you have said?
- ❏ d do something else?

Theme F
The time of our life

1 Using your time

Draw a timetable for your week and show what you do at different times of the day.

- How much time do you spend in school?
- How much time do you spend on a hobby?
- How much time do you spend doing physical exercise?
- How much time do you spend relaxing?
- Do you think you waste any time?
- How can you use it more usefully?

Compare your timetable with other students.

2 Take a look at Theme F

Look at the pictures. Where can you find them in Units 16-18 and Option F?
Read the contents page. In which unit or units can you:

- read about Pelé and the history of football?
- revise the Passive?
- learn about parks in Canada?
- find out how people moved large stones 4000 years ago?
- discuss the rules of a game?

Around the Theme

UNIT

16 TOPIC AND LANGUAGE
Free time
page 66

How do you spend your free time? Do you have any hobbies? Do you like sport? Read about the different ways in which sport is important. Learn about Pele, the best footballer in the world. You can also revise the passive in English.

17 OUT AND ABOUT
The volleyball team
page 70

Is it all right for the volleyball team to break the rules? Lin doesn't think so. What do you think?

18 REVISION
page 72

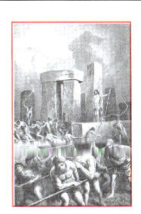

Revise the vocabulary and grammar that you learned. Learn how they built Stonehenge and ideas for protecting the countryside.

OPTION F CULTURE MATTERS
Discover Canada!
page 86

Canada has many magnificent national parks. Learn about some of the things that you can see and do there.

Free time activities; sport; the passive; teaching each other; curriculum links with Sport, Personal and Social Education

1 *Discussion*

2 *Listening*

3 *Discussion and reading*
IT A and B

Inside the text
A *Comprehension*
B *Vocabulary*

16 Free time
Topic and language

1 Hobbies and interests

1.1 In your free time

What hobbies or interests do you have? What do you like to do in your free time? Tell the class.

1.2 Types of free time activities

There are many different kinds of free time activities. We can put most of them into one of four different areas:

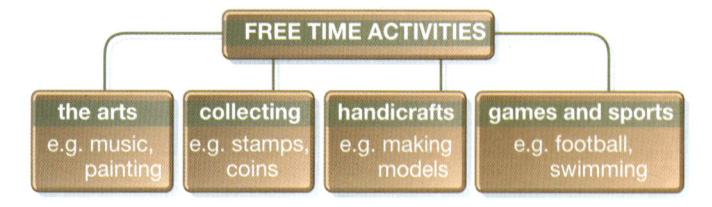

FREE TIME ACTIVITIES
- the arts e.g. music, painting
- collecting e.g. stamps, coins
- handicrafts e.g. making models
- games and sports e.g. football, swimming

Which area are you most interested in? Which areas are other people in your class interested in?

1.3 Some more hobbies and interests

In which area would you put these free time activities?

drama   computer graphics   computer games
singing   making furniture   mountain climbing

2 An unusual sport

2.1 Mick Hutton, taxi driver

Mick Hutton is a taxi driver in Cambridge, England. In his free time, he spends a lot of time on his sport. Listen. What is his sport? What exactly does he do?

Do you think it is an interesting hobby?

2.2 Listen again

Listen again and, with a neighbour, complete these notes.

Starting distance for training:
Distance in national competitions:
Distance in international competitions:
Usual speed (kph):
Maximum speed (kph):

What is the 'science' in Mick's hobby?

3 Sport for all

3.1 Do you like sport?

Some people love sport ... and some people hate it! Do you love it or hate it? Why? Are there some sports you like (or hate) more than others? Tell the class your ideas.

3.2 The value of sport

Sport is important for us in many ways. How? Work in a small group and brainstorm ideas. Compare your ideas with other students.

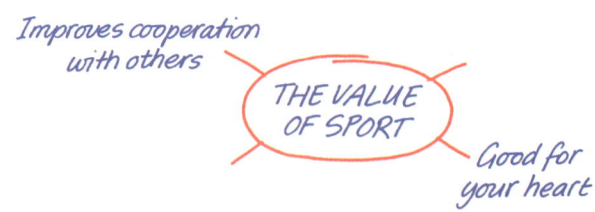

Improves cooperation with others

THE VALUE OF SPORT

Good for your heart

66   Free time

3.3 The changing nature of sport

In the past, sports were activities that people did for fun, in their free time. This has changed a lot in recent years. Read about some things that have changed.

- Do you think it is right to mix sport and politics?
- What do you think we should do about violence and sports?
- Do you think 'big business' has destroyed sport?

THE CHANGING NATURE OF SPORT

Sport provides entertainment for people all over the world. Millions of people practise sport and millions more follow their favourite sports personalities on television and radio or at games. But sport is important in other ways.

Sport and violence

In many countries, violence at football matches is a serious problem. In 1964, over 300 people were killed and more than 1000 people were injured when fans from Peru and Argentina started fighting. In 1985, in Brussels, Belgium, 38 people were killed and more than 200 were injured when fighting started between fans of the Liverpool (England) and Juventus (Italy) teams. As a result of that, England was not allowed in European football matches for five years.

Sport and politics

Sport has become closely connected with politics. In the 1970s and 1980s, for example, many people protested against sporting links with South Africa because of the system of apartheid there. As a result, many countries boycotted all games with South Africa. In the same way, the United States of America and 40 other nations boycotted the Olympic Games in Moscow in 1980 when Soviet armies entered Afghanistan. The Soviet Union then boycotted the following Olympics in Los Angeles, USA in 1984.

Sport and big business

Today, the sports industry is huge. Most big football clubs, for example, are run as businesses and aim to make a profit. Individual football players are promoted like film or pop stars, and they are then 'sold' to other clubs for millions of dollars. In 1981, for example, 20-year-old Diego Maradona of Argentina was sold by one club to another for $8 million. In 1997 the Brazilian player Ronaldo was sold for £18 million. On and off the field, sportspeople sometimes behave badly – often just to get attention.

Maradona transfer: $8 million

Record £15 million for Shearer

Ronaldo to Inter Milan – for £18 million!

Inside the text

A Check your understanding

Find these dates in the text. What happened on each date?

1964   1970s   1980s   1980   1981   1984
1985

Find these numbers in the text. What do they refer to?

200   40   20   38   5   1000   18 million pounds

B What's the word?

Match each word to the correct meaning.

1	provide (v.)	a	a system that separates black and white people
2	boycott (v.)		
3	apartheid (n.)	b	advertise
4	protest (v.)	c	enormous
5	following (adj.)	d	give
6	injure (v.)	e	hurt
7	fan (n.)	f	next
8	huge (adj.)	g	refuse to take part in something
9	promote (v.)	h	speak against something
		i	supporter

Unit 16   Topic and language

4 *The passive*
WB Ex. 2;

5 *Language record*

4 Language focus
Revision: the passive

4.1 Active and passive

It is possible to say many things in English in two ways. You can make an 'active sentence', for example:

> Owners of big football clubs run the clubs as businesses.
> They promote individual football players like film or pop stars.
> Clubs then 'sell' football players for millions of dollars.
> In 1997, a football club sold Ronaldo for £18 million.

Or you can make a 'passive sentence':

> Most big football clubs are run as businesses.
> Individual football players are promoted like film or pop stars.
> They are then 'sold' to clubs for millions of dollars.
> In 1997, Ronaldo was sold for £18 million.

What differences can you see between the first and the second sets of sentences? How do you say those sentences in your language?

4.2 When can you use the passive?

The passive is often used in English when:

a the action is more important than who does it, or we don't know exactly who does it.
> Most big football clubs are run as businesses.

b you want to describe a process.
> Individual football players are promoted like film or pop stars. They are then 'sold' to clubs for millions of dollars.

c you want to write a rule.
> England was not allowed in European football matches for five years.

Read about volleyball. Is each sentence or group of sentences an example of a, b or c?

VOLLEYBALL

One of the world's most popular games.

[1] Volleyball is played all over the world. [2] It was invented in the United States of America in 1895.

[3] In the game, a ball is hit backwards and forwards over a net. [4] The players are not allowed to catch or throw the ball. They can only hit it.

[5] To start the game, the ball is served over the net to the other team. [6] The other team is not allowed to hit the ball more than three times before they return it. [7] If the ball is hit on to the floor of the opposing team, the serving team receives a point.

[8] A game is usually completed when one team scores 15 points, with at least 2 points more than the other team. [9] Volleyball competitions are played in sets of three or five games.

4.3 How to form the passive

How can you describe the *form* of the passive? Copy and complete the table with the other sentences from Exercise 4.2.

Subject	+ _____	+ _____
Most clubs	are	run …
England	was	allowed …

68   Free time

4.4 PRACTICE

Read about the history of football and one of the world's greatest players – Pelé from Brazil. Can you complete the text with the correct form of the verb? (Check with the list of irregular verbs on page 90.)

PELÉ and THE HISTORY OF FOOTBALL

Football is the most popular game in the world.

It ¹.................... first .... (play) in England in the early 1800s. In the beginning, the rules ² .... (change) many times, but in 1863 the Football Association ³.................... .... (form) to agree a set of rules.

In 1904 the Fédération Internationale de Football Association (FIFA) ⁴.................... .... (form). The first World Cup competition ⁵.................... .... (organise) by FIFA in 1930. It ⁶.................... .... (play) in Uruguay. Since then it has been played every four years, except during World War II when it ⁷.................... .... (suspend).

Probably the greatest player in the history of football was Pelé, from Brazil. When Pelé was just 15 he ⁸.................... .... (choose) by the football club Santos. A year later, at 16, he ⁹.................... .... (select) for the national team, and in 1958 he played in the World Cup. Brazil won the Cup, by defeating Sweden 5 - 2. Two of Brazil's goals ¹⁰.................... .... (score) by Pelé. Brazil won the World Cup again in 1962 but they ¹¹.................... .... (defeat) in 1966. In 1970, Brazil won the Cup again, with Pelé on the team.

Pelé was the only professional footballer to score more than 1,000 goals (1,281 goals in 1,363 games). He retired in 1974 but in 1975 he ¹².................... .... (pay) $4 million to play for a New York team. He retired again in 1977. Today he is still a national hero in Brazil.

5 Your Language Record

5.1 Your Grammar Record

Make notes in your *Grammar Record* about how to form and use the passive in English. Look at Exercise 4 and the *Language summaries* in your Workbook for ideas.

5.2 Your Record of Language Use

Look back at the Unit. Are there more words or phrases you want to add to your *Record of Language Use*?

Nouns ability   apartheid   coin   competition   computer graphics   distance   drama   entertainment   fan   free time   furniture   goal   handicrafts   hero   hobby   knowledge   match   net   pigeon   politics   profit   rule   speed   stamp   the arts   violence

Verbs aim   allow   behave   boycott   climb   collect   follow (a team)   injure   promote   protest   retire   run (a business)   score   serve (a ball)

Adjectives huge   maximum   serious   usual

Prepositions between

Adverbs as a result   backwards   badly   forwards   just

Time to spare?

Choose one of these exercises.

1 Look at the *Help yourself list* on pages 91–2. Make an exercise about this Unit.

2 Imagine that you meet someone who doesn't know anything about your favourite sport or hobby. What can you tell them? Write one or two paragraphs.

3 Imagine you are going to interview your favourite sports star. Write some questions. Find a partner and act out the interview.

The rights and wrongs of rules;
Present continuous for future reference

1 *Discussion*

2 *Listening and discussion*

3 *Present continuous*

4 a *Writing and speaking*
  b *Writing*
  c *You decide*

17 The volleyball team
Out and about with English

1 What do you think?

Discuss these questions with your class.

- Why do we have rules?
- Are some rules more important than other rules?
- Is it all right sometimes to ignore rules?

Look at these rules. Should you always follow them? Why/why not?

In football, you must not kick or push another player.

2 A volleyball competition

Listen to Part A of the conversation. Discuss these questions with a neighbour and then tell the class what you think.

- What does Lin think about the volleyball team?
- What does Tom think? Why does he say that Nick *has to* play?
- Do you think Nick should play in the team?

Listen to Part B.

- Lin says 'But that's against the rules.' What are the rules?
- Mr Johnson says 'But sometimes …'. What do you think he was going to say?

Read Lin's last sentence. What do you think?

Listen to Part C.

- When Mr Johnson says 'It's only a game,' what does he mean?
- Are rules the most important thing in a game?
- What do you think the volleyball team should do?

3 Inside the text
Present continuous

You can use the Present continuous to talk about:

a things that are happening *now*.
b fixed plans for the future.

Find these sentences in the text. Are they examples of a or b?

1 *I'm writing down* the times of the games tomorrow.
2 *Are you playing*?
3 *We're talking* about the volleyball team.
4 *He's playing* tomorrow.

Write a few sentences about your fixed plans for this week, this month and this year. Tell the class. For example:

I'm seeing my uncle on Saturday.

4 Decide …

Work by yourself or in a small group. Choose a, b, or c.

a What happened next?

What did Mr Johnson decide to do? How did he explain it to the team? What did he say to Nick? Prepare a conversation with Mr Johnson. Act it out for the class.

b Some good rules

Think about your school. What rules would make life easier and better for everyone? Write your own set of school rules.

c You decide!

Look at pages 91–2 for ideas. You could:

– make an exercise about this Unit.
– think about another situation where a rule is important. Prepare a conversation and act it out for the class.
– write a poem about the rules of life.

70 The volleyball team

The volleyball team

Part A

LIN: Hi, Tom. What are you up to?
TOM: Hi, Lin. I'm writing down the times of the games tomorrow. There's a volleyball competition for the Under 16 clubs.
LIN: Oh, right. Are you playing?
TOM: Of course!
LIN: Who else is in the team?
TOM: There's a list here. Look.
LIN: Steve, Otis, Ali, Nick ... Nick? He's not under 16!
TOM: Yes, he is.
LIN: No, he isn't, Tom. I went to his birthday party last Saturday. He was 16 last Saturday.
TOM: So what? OK, he's 16 and three days.
LIN: Well, that's not on, Tom. If he's 16 he's not *under* 16.
TOM: Look, Lin. Nick *has to* play. If he doesn't play, then nobody can play. We haven't got enough players for the team without him.
LIN: Does Mr Johnson know?
TOM: Of course he knows. He's our trainer.

Part B

LIN: And what does Mr Johnson say?
MR JOHNSON: What does Mr Johnson say about what, Lin?
TOM: Oh hello, Mr Johnson. We're talking about the volleyball team.
LIN: Well, Nick is in the team but he isn't under 16.
MR JOHNSON: I know. He's playing tomorrow but that's his last game with the team.
LIN: But that's against the rules, Mr Johnson.
MR JOHNSON: Yes, Lin. But sometimes ...
LIN: So, if I lie about my age so I can get a cheaper ticket on a bus, is that OK?

Part C

MR JOHNSON: No, Lin, it isn't. Stealing is wrong. That's very different.
LIN: Why is it different?
MR JOHNSON: Lin, I didn't want to include Nick, but I have to. If he doesn't play, then nobody will play. And if our team doesn't play, there won't be a tournament. It's only a game, Lin.
LIN: Exactly. A game is about trust. Tricking the other team isn't right. Rules are the most important thing in a game.
TOM: Lin, cool it! Don't get so worked up.
MR JOHNSON: Lin's got a point, Tom. Perhaps we ought to think about this again.
TOM: Oh no. Thank you, Lin. You've been a great help.

Idiom box

What are you up to? What are you doing?
So what? That's not important.
That's not on. That's not right or fair.
What's up? What's the problem?
Cool it! Calm down!
Don't get so worked up. Don't be so angry.

Revision of Units 13–17

1. *Self assessment*
2. *Vocabulary*
3. *'unless'*
4. *Second conditional*

18 Revision

1 How well do you know it?

How well do you think you know the English you learnt in Themes E and F? Put a tick (√) in the table.

	very well	OK	a little
Vocabulary			
Unless			
Second conditional			
Past passive			

2 The words you met

2.1 Word pairs

Here are some of the words you saw in Theme E (Units 13–15). The first word in each set is sometimes used with one of the words a–d. Can you match them? For example:

1. (endangered) a causeway   b myth   c (species)   d giant
2. natural   a culture   b resources c legend   d volcano
3. historic   a language   b copy   c column   d site
4. wide   a gaps   b designs   c movements   d rock formations
5. urgent   a place   b legend   c help   d future
6. preserve   a a design   b our history c a hut   d a mystery
7. geometric   a religion   b design   c characteristic   d influence

2.2 Complete the sentences

Now choose the correct word pair for each sentence.

a In the Great Rift Valley there are .... over 60 metres across.

b The columns of the Giant's Causeway in Northern Ireland seem to have a ....

c Machu Picchu, in Peru, is an example of an ....

d People probably abandoned Easter Island because they used all the ....

e If we want future generations to learn about their past, we have to ....

f The giant tortoises on the Galapagos Islands are an example of an ....

g Many other animals need .... so that they can survive.

3 There will be trouble unless …

Think of six things you must do (today, tomorrow or next week) and write about what will happen if you don't do them. For example:

Unless I go to bed now, I will wake up too late tomorrow morning.

4 Problems in the woods

Some students had a meeting to brainstorm some ideas about how to protect a wood and its animals. Read the notes and write a sentence for each one.

PROBLEMS
1. People drop rubbish everywhere.
2. People take their dogs into the woods.
3. People take birds' eggs.
4. People walk everywhere and destroy the plants.
5. Farm animals sometimes go into the woods.

IDEAS
Put rubbish bins in the woods.
Put up a sign 'No Dogs'.

Build boxes for birds.
Make some paths between the trees.
Build a fence.

If we put rubbish bins in the woods, people wouldn't drop rubbish everywhere.

5 *Second conditional*
5 *Past passive*

5 Our heritage

5.1 Your ideas

Imagine that you were responsible for the heritage of your country. What would you do in these situations?

1 Builders discover a 5000-year-old city where they are building a new road.
   If builders discovered an old city ....

2 Divers discover an old civilisation under the sea near your country.

3 Farmers take stones from an ancient wall to rebuild their own walls.

4 People leave rubbish inside the most famous old building in your country.

5 Another country has many of your old paintings in its museums.

5.2 Things to see in your country

Where would you take someone if they came to see the history of your country? Write some ideas about what you would show them in the north, the south, the east and the west.

If someone came to see the history of my country, I would first take them to .... There, they would see ...

6 How was Stonehenge built?

Read about how they built Stonehenge. Can you complete the text with the correct form of the passive?

Stonehenge is a group of enormous stones in the south of Britain. The stones all stand in a circle. Archaeologists think that work [1] *was started* (start) on Stonehenge about 5,000 years ago. They think that, first, one large stone [2] _____ (place) in the centre of a circle and then many wooden posts [3] _____ (put) into the ground around it. Later, many different kinds and sizes of stones [4] _____ (bring) from other parts of the country. Eighty-two huge bluestones [5] _____ (transport) from South Wales by boats.

Other stones, weighing more than 50 tonnes, [6] _____ (pull) 30 kilometres across the land on carts. The stones [7] _____ (shape) with stone tools and then levers [8] _____ (use) for the first time to lift the stones into position. Why did they do it? No one is sure. Some archaeologists say that it [9] _____ (make) as a calendar so that the local people would know when to plant their crops. Other historians say that it [10] _____ *(design) as a* religious temple. Stonehenge is another of history's mysteries.

Unit 18   Revision   75

Evaluation | Grammar

1 Looking at grammar

1.1 Grammar and you

Work by yourself. Answer the questions in the questionnaire.

Compare your answers with other students in your class.

1.2 Grammar in the classroom

Look back at the grammar you did in Theme F. What problems did you have?

Was it difficult or easy to remember and use?

Did you enjoy using it? Why/why not?

How can you improve the way you learn grammar?

Write about your ideas and give your paper to your teacher. (You don't have to put your name on it.)

1.3 Be independent!
Improve your grammar!

Work in pairs or a small group. Brainstorm some ways you can get extra grammar practice.

What can you do? For example: you can correct each other's grammar mistakes, you can make 'grammar posters' to put on the classroom wall, write down a favourite song in English and make a list of the grammar structures in it …

Tell your teacher your ideas. Agree when you can do it, in class or at home.

Questionnaire
Grammar

1 When you learn some new grammar, do you:
- ❏ a compare it with the grammar of your own language?
- ❏ b compare it with some other part of English grammar?
- ❏ c learn some example sentences by heart?
- ❏ d do something else?

2 While you are learning some new grammar, do you:
- ❏ a look at the language summaries?
- ❏ b look in another grammar book?
- ❏ c write some example sentences with translations in your Grammar Record?
- ❏ d write some example sentences on cards with translations on the back?
- ❏ e change some sentences from an old structure to the new one?
- ❏ f something else?

3 While you are practising a new grammar structure, do you:
- ❏ a expect to make mistakes?
- ❏ b compare your mistakes with other students?
- ❏ c get worried if you make a mistake?
- ❏ d like to do a lot of grammar exercises?
- ❏ e like to work out the grammar yourself?
- ❏ f do something else?

4 When you have learned a new grammar structure, do you:
- ❏ a use it as often as you can?
- ❏ b look and listen out for the structure in other texts?
- ❏ c try to avoid using it because you think you'll make a mistake?
- ❏ d do something else?

2 A letter to you

Here is a letter to you, from the authors.

Dear Student

This is almost the end of the book! We hope that you have enjoyed using it and that it has helped you to improve your English. We also hope that the book has helped you to learn a lot of other things about the world.

Now that you have come to the end of the book, we would like to learn something from you! We would like to hear your opinions and ideas about this book. In that way, we can continue to improve the books that we write. Can you write to us and tell us what you think? Here are some questions:

Did you like the topics in the book?
What was your favourite topic?
What was your least favourite topic?
Did you find the exercises difficult, easy or just right?
Were there some types of exercises that you liked a lot?
Were there some types of exercises that you didn't like at all?
If there was another book after this, what topics would you like in it?

Please also tell us something about yourself:

How old are you?
How long have you been studying English?

Many thanks! We look forward to hearing from you.

Best wishes

Andrew Littlejohn and Diana Hicks
(authors)

Andrew Littlejohn and Diana Hicks,
c/o ELT Group,
Cambridge University Press,
The Edinburgh Building,
Shaftesbury Road,
Cambridge CB2 2RU,
England.

Work by yourself or in a small group. Think about your answers to our questions and write to us!

You can also send a fax to:

++ 44 1223 325984

Or you can send us an email message to

aldh@cup.cam.ac.uk

Many thanks – and good luck!

To: aldh@cup.cam.ac.uk
Subject: Level 4

Dear Andrew and Diana
We are students at a school in

Evaluation 77

Discussion about friendship; describing objects and past actions;

1 *Discussion*
2 *Listening*
3 *Language focus*
4 *Speaking and writing*

A OPTIONAL UNIT
A friend in need
Out and about with English

1 What do you think?

Discuss these questions with your class.

Is it always wrong to tell lies?
Do you know what a 'white lie' is?
Are some lies worse than others?

Look at the pictures. What do you think is happening?

2 Who did it?

2.1 A beautiful bag

Samantha and Rebecca are alone in the classroom. They are looking at their teacher's bag. Listen to Part A. Why do they like the bag? What happens to it? Why is Samantha so worried?

What should Rebecca and Samantha do next?

2.2 What have you done?

Listen again to Part B. How does Mrs Wilson know they have touched her bag? What does Rebecca do for Samantha?

Did Rebecca do the right thing?
What do you think is going to happen to Rebecca?
What is more important – being a good friend or not lying?
Have you ever been in a situation like that?

3 Inside the text
Present perfect and Future simple

Look back through the dialogue in Exercise 2.

How many examples of the Present perfect ('have' + past participle) and the Future simple ('will') can you find? You can also use 'will' to make offers. For example, Samantha says to Rebecca:

I'll get you one for your birthday.

Can you find two more offers in the dialogue?

4 Decide …

Work by yourself or in a small group. Choose a, b or c.

a With the head teacher

Read through Exercise 2 again.
What happened in the head teacher's office? Prepare a short play. Act it out for the class or record it on a cassette.

b Letter to a friend

Imagine that Rebecca wrote a letter to another friend. She told her friend what happened and why she helped Samantha. Write Rebecca's letter.

c You decide!

Look at page 91–2 for ideas. You could:
- write a poem about friendship.
- write a story where a friend is important.
- write about your best friend.

Theme A

Protecting a friend

Part A

SAMANTHA: Look at Mrs Wilson's bag, Becky. It's beautiful.
REBECCA: Wow. I'd love a bag like that.
SAMANTHA: I'll get you one for your birthday, if it's not too expensive.
REBECCA: Leave it alone, Sam.
SAMANTHA: Come on. Becky. Don't be silly. Let's have a look. It's got a pocket here and here. The material is really nice.
REBECCA: I wonder where she got it.
SAMANTHA: There's a name on the bottom. It says …
REBECCA: Watch out! Everything is falling out! Look what you've done!
SAMANTHA: Oh no!
REBECCA: Quick! I'll help you. Mrs Wilson's coming!
SAMANTHA: I'll get into terrible trouble with my parents if she finds out.

Part B

MRS WILSON: Hello, girls. What are you doing here?
REBECCA: Nothing, Miss. Just talking.
MRS WILSON: Are you sure? You both look very strange to me.
SAMANTHA: I'll help you with the books, Miss.
MRS WILSON: That's OK. Go back to your desks. The class is coming in now.
REBECCA: Yes, Miss.

MRS WILSON: Samantha! Rebecca! Come here! Have you opened my bag?
SAMANTHA: No, Miss.
MRS WILSON: Then why is my purse on the floor?
REBECCA: Don't know, Miss.
MRS WILSON: Well, we're going straight to the head teacher. She can find out. Come on!
SAMANTHA: No, Miss, please! My parents will be furious if I get into trouble with the head.
MRS WILSON: That's your problem. Come on. Now.
REBECCA: Wait, Mrs Wilson, wait. Samantha hasn't done anything, Miss. It was me.
MRS WILSON: What do you mean?
REBECCA: Sam was working at her desk. I picked up your bag and looked at it. Everything fell out.
MRS WILSON: Samantha, is this true?
SAMANTHA: Er, well, er …
MRS WILSON: Rebecca. Come with me. We're going to see the head. Samantha, get on with your work.
SAMANTHA: Er, Yes, Miss. OK, Miss. Becky!

Idiom box

I'd love …   I would like to have …
Leave it alone   Do not touch it.
Come on!   Let's go/do it
really nice   very nice
Watch out!   Be careful
straight   directly
Get on with…   Continue to do something

Optional Unit   79

Creative writing

OPTIONAL UNIT B
Write a story
Fluency

1 Another world

1.1 In your imagination

Imagine … another world, another time, another place. Work by yourself. Think about these questions and note down some ideas.

Compare ideas with a neighbour.

- Is it on Earth, on another planet, or in space?
- Is it in the past, present or the future?
- Is it on land, in the air, or on the sea?
- What does it feel like to be there? Is it a friendly place?
- What is the climate like? Is it hot or cold? Wet or dry?
- What does it look like? Is it light or dark?

Another world

1.2 A person

Now imagine that there is a person in that place. Think of some more answers.

- Is it a man or a woman?
- What is the person doing?
- Why is the person there?
- How does the person feel about the place?
- What is the person intending to do next?
- Suddenly … what happens?

1.3 Write!

Write about your ideas.

a **Write a draft:** For example, you could write the beginning of a short story, or a poem or a diary. Make changes as you write.

> The ~~empty~~ surface of the planet was ~~cold~~ and the wind was blowing across the dry open plains. Alone, Hari Jun was doing some simple repairs to his ~~space rocket~~ spacebike. Hari Jun was about 134 years old. At least he thought he was about that old. He couldn't remember exactly because…

> Standing in the sun,
> Suzi could feel the heat ~~on her skin.~~
> Her eyes were closed.
> Her head up, the wind on her skin.
> She was thinking.

b **Check it:** Read through your work and check: spelling grammar vocabulary style

c **Revise it:** Exchange your work with other students. Can you suggest improvements to each other's work?

d **Finalise it:** Look at your work and write a final version.

e **Publish it!** You can collect your work together and make a poster or a booklet with your class work.

OPTIONAL UNIT
USA – a melting pot
Culture matters

C

The peoples of the United States
Fluency practice

1. *A writing game*
2. *Reading*
3. *Listening and discussion*
4. *Research and writing*

1 What do you know?

Play a quick game about the United States. Work in a small group. You have four minutes. Write down as much as you know under each heading.

- Cities: Washington
- States: Colorado
- Natural features: Mississippi river
- Famous people:
- Recent events:
- Industries:

When the time is finished, compare with other groups.

2 The Americans

2.1 Who lives in the United States?

Look at the photographs of the people. Which countries do you think they or their ancestors came from originally? Make a list.

Today, there are about 250 million Americans. Guess! Draw a pie chart and write the percentages of people from each country.

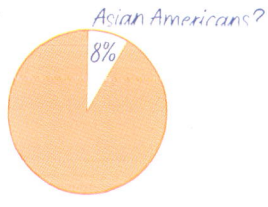

Asian Americans? 8%

2.2 A melting pot

Are you right? Read about the population of the United States. Draw another pie chart and fill in the information in the article.

A melting pot

The United States of America has probably one of the most 'mixed' populations in the world. This is why it is often called 'a melting pot'.

The first Americans were the Native Americans – there are about 2 million of them today, about 0.8% of the population. Their ancestors came to America over a 'land bridge' from Asia 40,000 years before Columbus.

The Europeans arrive

Many, many years later, in the 1600s, people arrived from Europe. The first groups came from England and France. Today about 32 million Americans (about 13%) have English ancestors from over 300 years ago.

The Europeans also took people by force from Africa to work for them in the 'New World'. As slaves they had a very hard and difficult life, and many of them died during the journey to America or on tobacco and cotton farms. There are about 30 million black Americans (about 12% of the population) in the United States today and most of these are descendants of slaves.

More recently, people have come to the United States from other parts of the world. Between 1820 and 1860 many people came from Germany and Ireland – about 58 million (about 23%) of Americans have German ancestors, and about 39 million (15%) have Irish ancestors. From 1860 to 1920 many more people came from other European countries including Russia, Poland, Greece, Turkey and Italy.

The USA today

Today, the fastest growing group in the United States is Hispanic. There are about 25 million Hispanics (about 9% of the population) in the United States who come from Spanish-speaking countries such as Cuba, Mexico and Puerto Rico. There are also large numbers of people from Asian countries, including China, Japan, Korea and the Philippines. In total, there are about 7.5 million Asian Americans (about 3% of the population).

3 Slavery, a crime against humanity

3.1 The life of a slave

Read about slavery in the United States.

> Slavery existed in the United States for hundreds of years, until 1865. Slaves had no rights at all – they were the property of their owners. They lived in very bad conditions, received minimal amounts of food and were treated very badly. Many slaves tried to escape but, if they were caught, they were punished very hard.

Look at the pictures. How would you feel if you were a slave? What would you do?

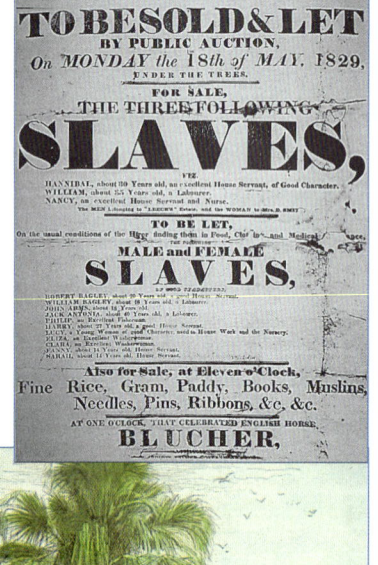

3.2 A long journey

Many black Americans are now trying to find where their ancestors came from. Listen. Janis Harvey is talking about her family history. What happened on these dates? Work with a partner. One of you choose list A, the other list B. Note down your answers.

List A: 1985 1845 1865
List B: 1870 1834 1996

Listen again. Check your partner's notes.

4 Decide ... Across cultures

Choose **a** or **b**.

a **The population of your country**
Find out about different groups of people in your country. Where did they come from? Where do they live? What languages do they speak? Can you make pie charts to show your information?

b **Your country and the United States**
Have many people from your country gone to live in the United States? Where did they go? What did they do there? Ask your friends, family and teachers. Write about what you discover.

OPTIONAL UNIT

A letter for the world

Fluency

D

1 *Discussion and letter writing*

1 A letter for the world

1.1 World leaders

Who decides our future, do you think? Which world leaders make decisions that affect us all? With your class, make a list.

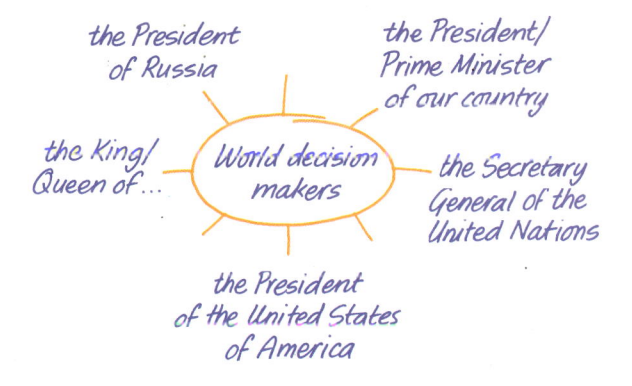

World decision makers:
- the President of Russia
- the President/Prime Minister of our country
- the King/Queen of ...
- the Secretary General of the United Nations
- the President of the United States of America

1.2 Your ideas for the future

If you could talk to a world leader, what would you say? Note down your ideas.

- What problems for the future would you talk about?
- What would you ask them to do *now* to protect the future?
- What good things do we need to preserve?
- What can you tell them about your hopes?
- What do other students think?

1.3 A letter to a world leader

Work in a small group. Choose one of the people you listed in Exercise 1.1 and plan a letter to that person. Follow these steps.

a **Plan:** Talk about what you want to write.

b **Write a draft:** Decide exactly what you can say in your letter. Together, write a draft about each idea (everybody in the group must write). OR Decide who will write each section, and work individually. Help each other with spelling, grammar, vocabulary and phrasing. Ask your teacher for help.

c **Check it:** Read through your work and check: spelling   grammar   vocabulary   style

d **Revise it:** Exchange your work with other students. Can you suggest improvements to other students' letters?

e **Finalise it:** Look at the letter outline and write the final version.

f **Post it:** Your teacher has some addresses.

Your address
Country
Date

Name and address
of the person
you are writing to

Dear Name of person

We are students in ... and we are writing to you to tell you about our ideas about the future. We hope that you can spare a few minutes to read what we have written.

At the moment ... We think ...
We are worried that ... We hope that ...
Thank you very much for your attention.

With best wishes

Your names

Optional Unit 83

Discussion about charity; making comparisons

1. *Discussion*
2. *Listening*
3. *Language use*
4. *Decide …*

OPTIONAL UNIT
A sponsored fast
Out and about with English

1 What do you think?

Look at the pictures and objects. Discuss these questions with your class.

- Is it always good to give money to poorer people?
- Is it better to give the money to organisations?
- Have you ever given money to anyone? Who? Why?
- Have you ever given money to an organisation? Which one? Why?

2 Give me some money!

2.1 The sponsored fast

Samantha is asking her school friends to sponsor her – to say that they will give her some money for charity. Listen to Part A. What is Samantha going to do? Why?

What do you think of Samantha's idea?
Have you ever been sponsored for a charity?
Have you ever fasted for 24 hours?

2.2 What's it for?

Listen to Part B. Why is Samantha going to fast?

Would you sponsor Samantha? Do you agree with Blake and Steve? Do you think Samantha should fast for people and animals, not old buildings? Do you think charity should 'begin at home'?

3 Inside the text
Past passive

Read the conversation again. How many examples of the Past passive and the second conditional can you find? Add the examples to your *Record of Language Use*.

4 Decide …

Work by yourself or in a small group. Choose **a**, **b**, or **c**.

a What happens next?

Read the second part of the conversation again. What do you think Samantha is going to say next? Work with a partner or in a small group and continue the dialogue. Act out your dialogue or record it.

b A charity poster

Think of a charity which you support. Design a poster that asks people to go on a 15-kilometre sponsored run. People will run in every large town in the world on the same day at the same time.

c You decide!

Look at page 91–2 for ideas. You could:

- write a song about people or places that need help. Choose a song you know and write some new words. Sing it!
- write a poem about the rich and poor countries in the world.

Samantha asks for sponsors

Part A

SAMANTHA: Come on, everyone! Come and sponsor me!
BLAKE: What for, Samantha?
SAMANTHA: Well, I'm going to fast for 24 hours.
STEVE: You mean you're not going to eat for 24 hours! No breakfast, no delicious school lunch …
BLAKE: Why?
REBECCA: Are you *sure* you can do it, Samantha?
SAMANTHA: Well, don't all speak at once! I'm not sure if I can or I can't. There's a group of us doing it …
BLAKE: What for?
SAMANTHA: It's for charity … it's an organisation.
REBECCA: So, if I sponsored you for 24 hours, how much would that be?
SAMANTHA: Well, that depends. You can either give me a certain sum of money for every hour or …
STEVE: Depends on what?
SAMANTHA: … or you promise that you will give me a certain sum of money if I fast for 24 hours.
REBECCA: Sounds great, Samantha. I'll sponsor you 10p for every hour … where shall I sign?
SAMANTHA: Great, thanks, Rebecca … what about the rest of you?

Part B

BLAKE: So, why are you doing this, Samantha?
SAMANTHA: I told you, it's for charity.
BLAKE: I know – it's a 'Save the dolphin' charity, isn't it?
REBECCA: No, it isn't. Look, Blake, it's all written here.
SAMANTHA: It's to raise money for a really old temple in South America which was damaged by an earthquake last year.
STEVE: You're collecting money for an old building!
BLAKE: What about collecting money for people or animals?
STEVE: If you fasted for people I would sponsor you, but an old place …
BLAKE: I agree … Anyway, there are many people here in this country that need help. Why South America?
STEVE: Or what about the animals which were threatened by the drought in Africa last month?
BLAKE: I think if we give to charity we should help people or animals.
SAMANTHA: I can see that, but the point is …

Idiom box

Come on, everyone! Let's do it
Thats depends. It depends on a number of different things
Sounds great. That seems a good idea
The point is The reason is
Great, thanks Excellent, thank you
I can see that I understand that
Don't all speak at once! Why is everyone so quiet

Optional Unit 85

Famous places in your country and in Canada
Fluency practice

1 *Discussion*
2 *Reading*
3 *Listening*

OPTIONAL UNIT
Discover Canada!
Culture matters

1 Famous places in your country

If some visitors came to your country, which places would you take them to see? Why? Which places in your country would *you* like to visit? Tell the class your ideas.

2 Famous places in Canada

2.1 Places to visit

Look at the pictures of the famous places in Canada on these pages. Which places would you like to visit? Why?

2.2 Places and stories

Every picture tells a story, but one place can tell us hundreds of stories. Read some stories about some of Canada's parks.

Which parks would you visit if you wanted to:

- hear stories about the Blackfoot culture?
- see a village that is over 1,000 years old?
- see a bear?
- see tepees?
- see the first metal tools in North America?
- see high waterfalls?

1 Anthony Island Provincial Park

2 Wood Buffalo National Park

Rocky Mountain National Park

3 Quebec City

4 Kluane National Park

5

6 Dinosaur Provincial Park

L'Anse aux Meadows

L'Anse aux Meadows

On a summer's day nearly 1,000 years ago, a ship from Greenland arrived in Newfoundland, Canada. Leif Eriksson, the captain and his crew liked the warm climate and they decided to stay. They called the region 'Vinland' – the land of wine.

The Skraelings, who were probably Native Canadians, came to fight the Scandinavians. The Scandinavians left the region and moved to another part of Newfoundland – L'Anse aux Meadows – where they built houses and workshops. This was the first time that metal was made in the 'New World'. We don't know when they left but with time, grass grew over their houses and workshops.

In 1960, a Norwegian explorer – Helge Instad – found the 'village' and many things which were made by the Scandinavians. Today archaeologists are still discovering more about life here 1,000 years ago.

Head Smashed-In

For over 10,000 years the Native Canadian people and the buffalo lived together in the plains of Alberta. The Blackfoot was one of the Native Canadian tribes. They used the buffaloes for meat, clothes and for making tepees. They hunted the buffaloes by chasing them over high cliffs.

Head Smashed-In

About 150 years ago, a young Blackfoot wanted to watch the buffalo falling over the cliff so he stood in a small space inside the cliff. The pile of dead buffaloes became higher and higher. The young man couldn't move from his small space and he was killed. When the other men moved the buffaloes they found the young Blackfoot between the cliff and the buffaloes, with his head smashed in.

Nahanni National Park

Nahanni National Park

The South Nahanni River runs for 322 kilometres. It has many high waterfalls and dangerous rapids. It is a river of legends. Nearly a hundred years ago many people came here to look for gold. It was a dangerous place. Bears and wolves live in the valleys and the rapids can carry people away in seconds. Many people died mysteriously when they were looking for gold in the river – some disappeared in the river mist. When other adventurers found headless bodies in the river they called the area 'Deadmen Valley' and 'Headless Creek'.

3 Where are they?

Listen. A Canadian tourist guide is talking about some more places in Canada. What does she say you can do in each park? Make some notes about each place.

Quebec City: *see soldiers' uniforms from 300 years ago*
L'Anse aux Meadows:
Gros Morne Park:
Nahanni National Park:
Kluane National Park:
Rocky Mountain Park:
Wood Buffalo Park:
Anthony Island:

Which activities would you like to do?

A heritage map of the world

8 The Grand Canyon (USA)

18 Iguazú/Iguaçu National Park (Argentina/Brazil)

Some World Heritage Sites

1. Kluane National Park (Canada)
2. Anthony Island National Park (Canada)
3. Nahanni National Park (Canada)
4. Rocky Mountain National Park (Canada)
5. Dinosaur Provincial Park (Canada)
6. Head-Smashed-In (Canada)
7. Wood Buffalo National Park (Canada)
8. Grand Canyon National Park (USA)
9. El Tajin, Pre-Hispanic City (Mexico)
10. Galapagos Islands National Park (Ecuador)
11. Maya Ruins of Copan (Honduras)
12. Portobello and San Lorenzo Fortifications (Panama)
13. Quito (Ecuador)
14. Huascaran National Park (Peru)
15. Los Glaciares National Park (Argentina)
16. Quebec City (Canada)
17. Potosi (Bolivia)
18. Iguazú/Iguaçu National Park (Argentina/Brazil)
19. L'Anse aux Meadows Historic Park (Canada)
20. Historic Centre of Salvador de Bahia (Brazil)
21. Olinda (Brazil)
22. Evora (Portugal)
23. Alhambra (Spain)
24. The Giant's Causeway (UK)
25. Timbuktu (Mali)
26. Stonehenge (UK)
27. Hadrian's Wall (UK)
28. Arles (France)
29. Palaces and Parks of Potsdam and Berlin (Germany)
30. Venice (Italy)
31. Dja Faunal Reserve (Cameroons)
32. Spissky Hrad (Slovak Republic)
33. Kutna Hora (Czech Republic)
34. Rock Carvings in Tanum (Sweden)
35. Cracow Historic Centre (Poland)
36. Hollokö Traditional Village (Hungary)
37. Budapest (Hungary)
38. Plitvice Lakes National Park (Croatia)
39. Temple of Apollo Epicurius at Bassae (Greece)
40. Ivanovo Rock-hewn Churches (Bulgaria)

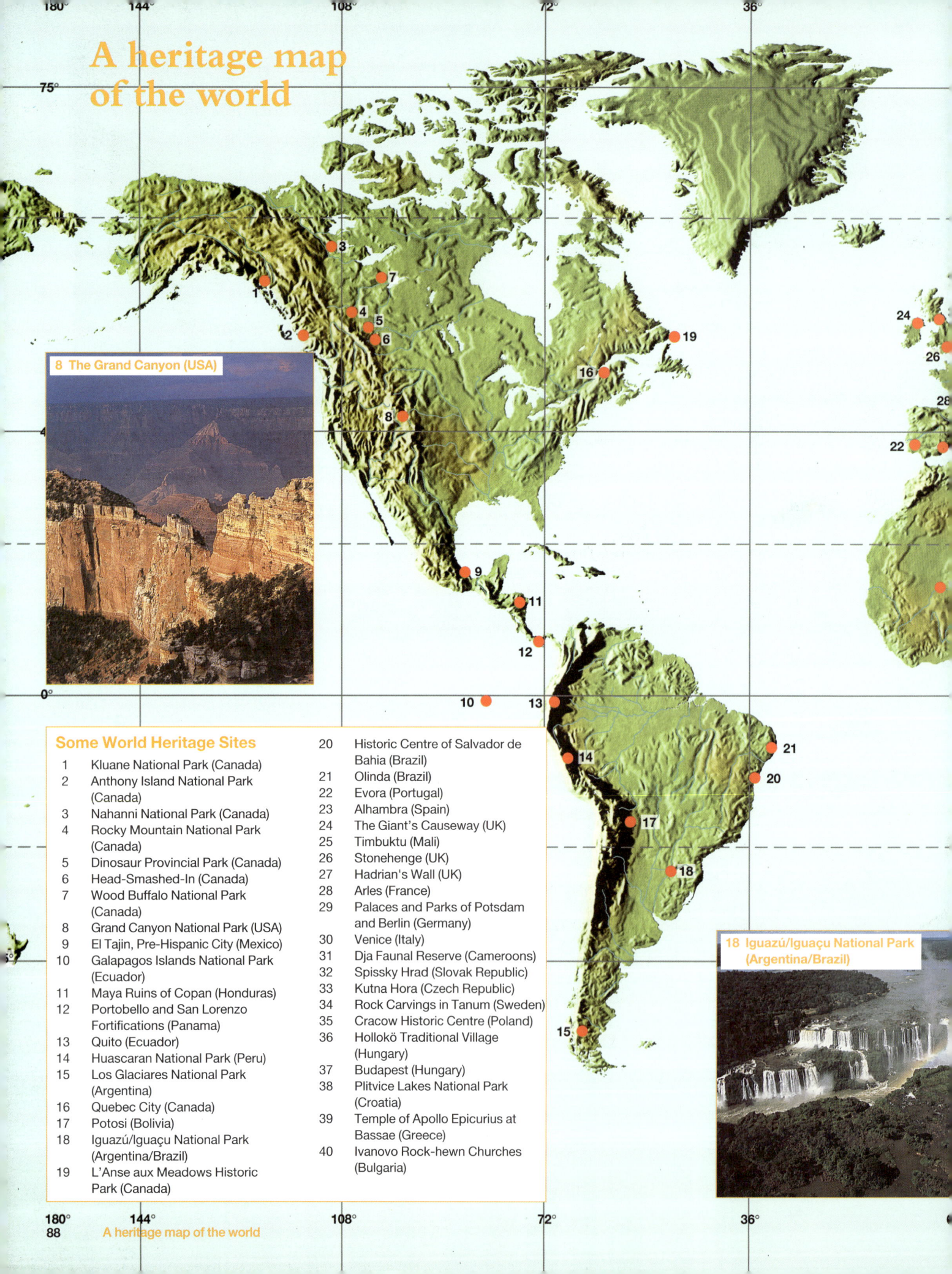

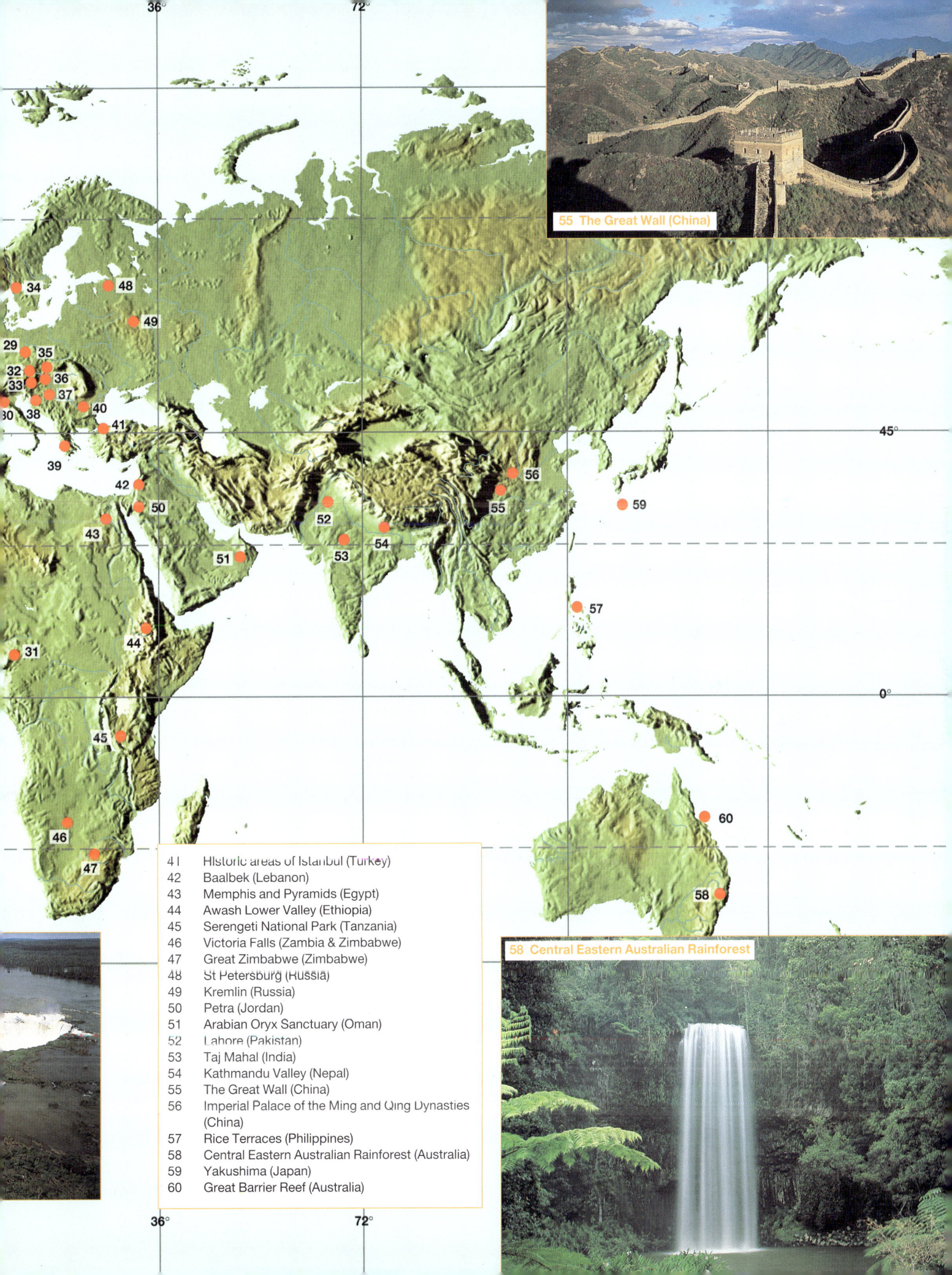

41	Historic areas of Istanbul (Turkey)
42	Baalbek (Lebanon)
43	Memphis and Pyramids (Egypt)
44	Awash Lower Valley (Ethiopia)
45	Serengeti National Park (Tanzania)
46	Victoria Falls (Zambia & Zimbabwe)
47	Great Zimbabwe (Zimbabwe)
48	St Petersburg (Russia)
49	Kremlin (Russia)
50	Petra (Jordan)
51	Arabian Oryx Sanctuary (Oman)
52	Lahore (Pakistan)
53	Taj Mahal (India)
54	Kathmandu Valley (Nepal)
55	The Great Wall (China)
56	Imperial Palace of the Ming and Qing Dynasties (China)
57	Rice Terraces (Philippines)
58	Central Eastern Australian Rainforest (Australia)
59	Yakushima (Japan)
60	Great Barrier Reef (Australia)

55 The Great Wall (China)

58 Central Eastern Australian Rainforest

Irregular verbs

Infinitive	Past simple	Past participle
be	was, were	been
become	became	become
begin	began	begun
bite	bit	bitten
blow	blew	blown
break	broke	broken
bring	brought	brought
build	built	built
buy	bought	bought
can	could	–
catch	caught	caught
choose	chose	chosen
come	came	come
cost	cost	cost
cut	cut	cut
dig	dug	dug
do	did	done
draw	drew	drawn
drink	drank	drunk
drive	drove	driven
eat	ate	eaten
fall	fell	fallen
feed	fed	fed
feel	felt	felt
fight	fought	fought
find	found	found
fly	flew	flown
forget	forgot	forgotten
forgive	forgave	forgiven
freeze	froze	frozen
get	got	got
give	gave	given
go	went	gone
grow	grew	grown

Infinitive	Past simple	Past participle
hang	hung	hung
have	had	had
hear	heard	heard
hide	hid	hidden
hit	hit	hit
hold	held	held
hurt	hurt	hurt
keep	kept	kept
know	knew	known
lay	laid	laid
lead	led	led
lean	leant	leant
leave	left	left
lend	lent	lent
let	let	let
lie	lay	lain
light	lit	lit
	lighted	lighted
lose	lost	lost
make	made	made
mean	meant	meant
meet	met	met
pay	paid	paid
put	put	put
read	read	read
ride	rode	ridden
ring	rang	rung
rise	rose	risen
run	ran	run
say	said	said
see	saw	seen
sell	sold	sold

Infinitive	Past simple	Past participle
send	sent	sent
set	set	set
shake	shook	shaken
shine	shone	shone
shoot	shot	shot
show	showed	shown
		showed
shut	shut	shut
sing	sang	sung
sink	sank	sunk
sit	sat	sat
sleep	slept	slept
slide	slid	slid
speak	spoke	spoken
spell	spelt	spelt
	spelled	spelled
spend	spent	spent
spread	spread	spread
stand	stood	stood
steal	stole	stolen
stick	stuck	stuck
sting	stung	stung
swim	swam	swum
swing	swung	swung
take	took	taken
teach	taught	taught
tell	told	told
think	thought	thought
throw	threw	thrown
understand	understood	understood
wake	woke	woken
wear	wore	worn
win	won	won
wind	wound	wound
write	wrote	written

Unit 8, Exercise 6.3 suggested answers

1 By 2050, the world population will have reached 10 billion.
2 By 2050, the population of China will have increased to 1.5 billion.
3 By 2050, the population of India will have grown to 1.6 billion.
4 By the year 2050, use of water will have grown to 24,000 cubic kilometres.
5 By 2050, they say the temperature of the Earth will have risen by 5°C.
6 Some scientists say that by 2010 the sea level will have risen by 9 cm compared to the sea level in 1970.

Help yourself list

Here are some ideas to give you more practice in English. You can work by yourself or with other students.

If you make an exercise for other students, remember to put the answers and your name on the back of the paper.

Closed exercises

These exercises have only one correct answer.

Ideas **Examples**

Idea 1 Fill in the missing words.

Choose a paragraph and take out some words.

Fill in the missing words.

> Space is not empty! Every week, more and more satellites are sent into space to orbit the Earth. A satellite usually works for about 10–12 years. Satellites which are broken are sometimes repaired by astronauts or sometimes they are brought back to the Earth to be repaired.

> Space is not empty! Every ...., more and more satellites are sent into .... to orbit the Earth. A satellite usually .... for about 10–12 years. Satellites which are .... are sometimes repaired by astronauts or sometimes they are brought back to the .... to be repaired.

Idea 2 Answer the questions

Choose a paragraph and write some questions.

Answer the questions.

> Space is not empty! Every week, more and more satellites are sent into space to orbit the Earth. A satellite usually works for about 10–12 years. Satellites which are broken are sometimes repaired by astronauts or sometimes they are brought back to the Earth to be repaired.

1 Who repairs the satellites in space?
2 What is the life span of a satellite?
3 What do satellites so in space?

Idea 3 True or false?

Choose a paragraph and write some true and false sentences.

Answer the questions.

> Space is not empty! Every week, more and more satellites are sent into space to orbit the Earth. A satellite usually works for about 10–12 years. Satellites which are broken are sometimes repaired by astronauts or sometimes they are brought back to the Earth to be repaired.

Are these sentences true, false, or is the information not in the text?

1 Every week more and more satellites are brought back to the Earth
2 A satellite usually lasts more than 12 years
3 Satellites can be repaired in space.

Idea 4 Listen and transcribe

Choose a small section from the cassette that is printed in your Student's Book or Workbook (look for ▭). Listen to it a few times and then try to write down what you hear.

Check your work with the text in the book.

> Lin: Hi, Tom. What are you up to?
> Tom: Hi, Lin I'm writing down the times of the games tomorrow. There's a volleyball competition for the Under 16 clubs.
> Lin: Oh, right. Are you playing?

Open exercises

These exercises are freer. There are many different answers and you can often use your imagination.

Ideas	Examples

Idea 5 Write a diary

Imagine you are somewhere special or that something unusual has happened. Write a page in a diary.

> March 11, 2050
> Yesterday was fantastic! I was on the first space plane that flew halfway around the world in two hours. There were about 400 people on the plane. There was a lot of room inside and we could walk around and look out of the windows. Outside, I could see …

Idea 6 Listen, and listen again

Choose something from your Workbook Cassette or record something in English from the radio or television (about two minutes in length). Listen to it all the way through and make some notes about what you remember. Leave lots of space between your notes. Listen again and again and try to complete your notes.

> Radio news
> 1 Earthquake in ?
>   2000 houses have been ?
>
> 2 President of Russia has met President of ?
>
> 3 Scientists have discovered a new ?

Idea 7 Prepare an interview

Think of a person and a situation. For example, a person who saw a crime, a famous pop singer, an astronaut, or an expert on something. Prepare some questions and some answers and act it out.

> A: Good afternoon, Mr Brown. You're a specialist on the effects of television. Could you tell us something about your research?
> B: Yes, well, it is a very difficult subject to research. Television, as we know, can have positive and negative effects.
> A: What are the positive effects?
> B: Well, TV can be very educational …

Idea 8 Write a radio or TV news report

You can write a radio or TV news report about the information in the Unit, or you can think of some news in your school, in your town or in the world. Use your imagination!

> Good evening. Here is the news for March 14 2099. Today the first commercial trip by Digital Human Transporter took place. The DHT is a revolutionary machine that converts people into electronic signals and transmits them to another place where they are converted back.
>   Fifty people travelled from …

Idea 9 Write about your favourite …

Think about the topics in the Units. Do you have a favourite story, book, singer, pop group, sport, hobby or film that you can write about? You can also include some pictures.

> My hobby: playing the guitar
> I started playing the guitar four years ago. I can play quite a few pop songs, although I can't sing very well. About six months ago, I began classical guitar lessons. I enjoy the lessons a lot, but practising makes my fingers hurt! Next December …

Wordlist/Index

In this list you can find the words which appear in the book and their page numbers. This is also an index of language areas and topics.

Abbreviations:
adj. adjective   *adv.* adverb   *exp.* expression
fem. feminine   *interj.* interjection   *n.* noun
prep. preposition   *pl.* plural   *sing.* singular   *v.* verb
Words *like this* are topics.

A

abandon *v.* 63
accident *n.* 19
accountant *n.* 23
act *v.* 19
active *adj.* 23
active and passive 68
actor *n.* (*fem.* actress) 22, 23
add up *v.* 24
administrative *adj.* 23
advertise *v.* 67
advice *n.* 26
afford *v.* 55
afraid *adj.* 31
against *prep.* 71
agree *v.* 69
agreement *n.* 32
agricultural *adj.* 15
agriculture *n.* 19
aid *n.* 15
aim *v.* 67
Alhambra *n.* 55
alkali *n.* 51
all at once *adv. exp.* 85
allow, be allowed to *v.* 44, 67
alternative *n.* 10
altitude *n.* 39
amount *n.* 19
Anasazi *n.* 63
ancestor *n.* 81
antenna *n.* (*pl.*antennae) 43
apartheid *n.* 67
archaeologist *n.* 63
architect *n.* 23
army *n.* 67
arts *n.* 66
as a result of *adv.* 67
astronaut *n.* 43
astronomer *n.* 23
Atlas mountains *n.* 39
at least *adv.* 68
atmosphere *n.* 10
attempt *n.* 10
attention *n.* 67
attract *v.* 22
author *n.* 77
average (*adv.*): on average 42
aware *adj.* 31

B

backwards *adv.* 68
badly *adv.* 67
bag *n.* 78, 79
balance *n.* 15
bank worker *n.* 23
bear *n.* 86
behave *v.* 67
behaviour *n.* 46
benefit *n.* 31
best-known *adj.* 10
between *prep.* 67
be up to something *idiom* 71
billion *n.* 31
birthday *n.* 78
Blackfoot *n.* 86
blind *adj.* 19
blow (blew, blown) *v.* 61, 80
boycott *v.* 67
brain *n.* 19, 31
broadcast *n.* 34
broken *adj.* 43
buffalo *n.* 86, 87
bulletin *n.* 35
by force *adv.* 82

C

calculator *n.* 24
camera *n.* 10
campsite *n.* 45
Canada 86
care (*v.*) for 58
carry (*v.*) away 87
catch *v.* 68
cause *n.* 19
causeway *n.* 59
ceremony *n.* 63
certain *adj.* 10, 84
chance *n.* 55, 62
channel *n.* 19, 35
charity 85
chef *n.* 23
China *n.* 21
cigarette *n.* 27
cleaner *n.* 11
climb *v.* 66
clone *n.* 19
cloud *n.* 43
coast *n.* 63
coin *n.* 66
coincidence *n.* 35
collect *v.* 66

collect *v.* 66
collection *n.* 59
colony *n.* 15
column *n.* 59
combination *n.* 22
commercial *adj.* 30
common *adj.* 15
communicate *v.* 11, 23
competition *n.* 66, 71
computer games n. 66
computer graphics n. 66
concert *n.* 11
concert hall *n.* 11
conditionals 26, 56
connect *v.* 19
connected *adj.* 39
connected with *adj.* 67
conquer *v.* 19
constant *adj.* 55, 59
construct *v.* 23, 63
construction *n.* 10
control *n.* 10
control *v.* 19
conversation *n.* 31
cool *v.* 59
Cool it! *idiom* 71
correspondent *n.* 36
crash *v.* 34, 43
create *v.* 23, 59
crime *n.* 31
critic *n.* 31
Cross my heart *idiom* 27

D

daily *adv.* 35
damage *v.* 55, 85
daytime *n.* 50
deaf *adj.* 19
decision *n.* 83
deep *adj.* 61
defeat *v.* 69
delicious *adj.* 85
deliver *v.* 45
demand *n.* 19
depend on *v.* 26
depth *n.* 19
descendant *n.* 82
destination *n.* 19
destroy *v.* 55, 67
development *n.* 10
device *n.* 19
did: *see Past simple* 33
dinosaur *n.* 33, 34

directly *adv.* 19
directory *n.* 24
disappear *v.* 19
discover *v.* 32
disease *n.* 19, 63
distance *n.* 66
doctor *n.* 22
dollar *n.* 67
dolphin *n.* 85
dominate *v.* 35
drama *n.* 66
driver *n.* 19
drought *n.* 85
dustbin *n.* 43
dye *n.* 51

E

earthquake *n.* 85
Easter Island *n.* 62, 63
economics *n.* 34
economy *n.* 15
effect *n.* 31
empty *adj.* 43
encourage *v.* 31
encyclopaedia *n.* 24
endangered *adj.* 58, 59
engineer *n.* 11, 23
enjoyable *adj.* 31
enormous *adj.* 10, 59, 63
entertain *v.* 31
entertainment *n.* 67
entry *n.* (*pl.* entries) 34
envelope *n.* 45
equator *n.* 43
equipment *n.* 10
erupt *v.* 12, 61
escape *v.* 82
especially *adv.* 23
estimate *v.* 31
exact *adj.* 45
exactly *adv.* 19, 71
except *adv.* 69
exist *v.* 19
expedition *n.* 10
expensive *adj.* 11
experience *n.* 49
experiment *v.* 23
export *v.* 19
export *n.* 15
express *v.* 23
extract *n.* 35

Wordlist   93

F

false *adj.* 31
famous *adj.* 54
fan *n.* 67
fantastic *adj.* 61
fast *n.* 85
fast *v.* 85
feedback *n.* 19
fence *n.* 55
field *n.* 67
FIFA *n.* 69
film star *n.* 67
find out *v.* 24
first conditional 14
follow *v.* 67, 70
following *adj.* 67
football *n.* 67, 69
Football Association *n.* 69
force *v.* 51
foreign *adj.* 34, 63
forget *v.* 32
form *v.* 69
forwards *adv.* 68
free time n. 66
friendship 78
fuel *n.* 19
furious *adj.* 79
furnace *n.* 51
furniture *n.* 66
future *n.* 18
Future simple 11, 14
Future perfect 21
futurologist *n.* 18
futurology *n.* 18

G

Galapagos Islands *n.* 59
game *n.* 70, 71
gardener *n.* 22
gene *n.* 19
geologist *n.* 59
get married *v.* 32
get up *v.* 24
get worked up *idiom* 71
giant *n. (fem.* giantess) 59
Giant's Causeway *n.* 59
glacier *n.* 59
global *adj.* 31
goal *n.* 69
going to 20
gold *n.* 87
gossip *n.* 35
government *n.* 10, 15
graffiti *n.* 56
grammar 76
grandchildren *n.* 55
Grandma *n.* 49
graph *n.* 23
greatest *adj.* 69
Great Rift Valley *n.* 61
Great Wall of China *n.* 55
Great Zimbabwe *n.* 62, 63
grow (grew, grown) *v.* 21
grow out of something *idiom* 27
guards *n.* 55
guide *n.* 55

H

habit *n.* 27
had done: *see Past perfect* 14
halfway *adv.* 19
handicrafts *n.* 66
has/have done: *see Present perfect* 32
have a point *v.* 71
have to *v.* 70
Head Smashed-In *n.* 87
headless *adj.* 87
hectare *n.* 63
height *n.* 19
hero *n.* 69
Heyerdahl, Thor *n.* 62
Hispanic people *n* 82
historic *adj.* 55
hit (hit, hit) *v.* 68
hobby *n.* 22, 66
hologram *n.* 19
holographic *adj.* 19
home *adj.* 34
housing *n.* 15
huge *adj.* 59, 67
hunger *n.* 63
hurt *v.* 26, 67
hut *n.* 63

I

ice *n.* 11
icehouse *n.* 11
I don't follow *idiom* 27
'if' sentences 26, 56
ignore *v.* 70
illegal *adj.* 27
image *n.* 18
imagination *n.* 80
immediately *adv.* 12
impressive *adj.* 63
improve *v.* 10
include *v.* 71
increase *v.* 19
independence *n.* 15
independent *adj.* 15
India *n.* 21
individual *adj.* 67
industry *n.* 67
injure *v.* 39, 67
install *v.* 55
instead *adv.* 19
intelligence *n.* 19
interesting *adj.* 54
international *adj.* 66
Internet *n.* 43
introduce *v.* 10
invent *v.* 68
iron age *n.* 63
isolated *adj.* 58, 59

J

job *n.* 9
join (*v.*) together 55
journalist *n.* 34
just *adv.* 67
Juventus *v.* 67

K

kill *v.* 59, 67
kiva *n.* 63
knock (*v.*) into 47

L

L'Anse aux Meadows *n.* 87
lake *n.* 10
land *v.* 19
land bridge *n.* 82
landscape *n.* 15
language record 9
large *adj* 10
lava *n.* 59
lawyer *n.* 23
lazy *adj.* 31
legend *n.* 59, 87
lemur *n.* 15
Let's *exp.* 47
letter writing 77
librarian *n.* 9, 22
lie *v*.: to tell lies 71
lift *v.* 59
light railway *n.* 10
link *n.* 67
listening 40
Liverpool *n.* 67
location *n.* 43
Loch Ness *n.* 10
log *n.* 51
look up *v.* 24
look (*v.*) after 55

M

Madagascar *n.* 15
magic *n., adj.* 30
Maglev train *n.* 10
Magnetic Levitation *n.* 10
maintain *v.* 55
Malaysia *n.* 15
Maradona, Diego *n.* 67
Mars *n.* 32
match *n.* 67
material *n.* 79
maximum *adj.* 66
medical *adj.* 19
melt *v.* 11
melting pot *n.* 81, 82
mend *v.* 22
menu *n.* 19
mill *n*.: paper mill 51
minimal *adj.* 82
missing *adj.* 39
mist *n.* 87
mix *v.* 67
model *n.* 66
Mongolia *n.* 39
monster *n.* 10
monument *n.* 55
moon *n.* 50
motor-cycle *n.* 49
mould *n.* 51
mountain climbing *n.* 66
move (*v.*) apart 61
movement *n.* 59
multi-storey *adj.* 63
murder *v.* 34
murderer *n.* 34
musician *n.* 23
mysterious *adj.* 63
mysteriously *adv.* 87
mystery *n.* 10
myth *n.* 59

N

Nahanni National Park *n.* 87
nation *n.* 67
national *adj.* 66
negative *adj.* 31
net *n.* 68
news *sing. n.* 32, 34
news presenter *n.* 22
night-time *n.* 50
North Pole *n.* 21
nurse *n.* 23

O

on to *prep.* 68
orbit *v.* 43
ordinary *adj.* 35, 43
organisation *n.* 55
organise *v.* 22, 69
ought to *v.* 71
owner *n.* 68, 82

P

painter *n.* 22
particularly *adv.* 59
pass *v.* 32
passage *n.* 63
passive *adj.* 31
Passive, Past passive 60
Passive, Present passive 44, 51, 68
Past actions- present result 32
Past continuous 10, 12
Past passive 60
Past perfect 11, 14
Past simple 10, 32
patience *n.* 23
patrol *v.* 55
pay rise *n.* 19
pattern *n.* 59
peak *n.* 39
Pelé *n.* 69
personality *n.* 67
photographer *n.* 23
phrasal verbs 24
physically *adj.* 23
pigeon *n.* 66
planet *n.* 32
Pluto *n.* 32
politician *n.* 22
politics *n.* 67
pollute *v.* 10
pollution *n.* 21
Pompei *n.* 12
pop concert *n.* 11
pop star *n.* 67
popular *adj.* 19
popularity *n.* 31, 42
positive *adj.* 31

94 Wordlist

post *n.* 45
postcode *n.* 45
pour *v.* 61
practical *adj.* 23
precise *adj.* 23
precisely *adv.* 48
predict *v.* 18
prediction *n.* 11, 18
prefer *v.* 21, 23
Present continuous 20, 70
Present passive 44, 51, 68
Present perfect 10, 32
preserve *v.* 55
president *n.* 32
Prime Minister *n.* 83
prime time *n.* 30
process *n.* 89
produce *v.* 19
professional *n.* 69
profit *n.* 67
programme *n.* 8, 19, 30
promise *v.* 27
promote *v.* 67
protect *v.* 55, 59, 62, 83
protest *n.* 67
provide *v.* 67
public *adj.* 10
Pueblo Bonito *n.* 62, 63
pull (*v.*) apart 61
pulp *n.* 51
punish *v.* 82
purse *n.* 79

Q

question tags 36, 49
questionnaire *n.* 39

R

raft *n.* 63
raise *v.*: raise money 85
rapid *n.* 87
rare *adj.* 58
rating *n.* 30
raw *adj.* 49
ray *n.* 54
reading 52
receive *v.* 68
recovery *n.* 35
refuse *v.* 67
relative clauses 11, 15
relax *v.* 31
remove *v.* 51
renovation *n.* 55, 62
repair *n., v.* 55
repair *v.* 13, 23, 43
repetitive *adj.* 36
replace *v.* 19
represent *v.* 63, 83
research *n.* 23, 31
researcher *n.* 31
respect *v.* 55
responsibility *n.* 23, 31
restore *v.* 55
retire *v.* 69
return *v.* 68
rise *n.* 21

risk *n.* 23
robot *n.* 19
rock formation *n.* 59
roof *n.* 63
rotate *v.* 43
rule *n.* 69, 70
run *v.* 61
run (a business) *v.* 67
run away *v.* 26

S

sail *v.* 13
salesperson *n.* 23
satellite *n.* 42, 43
schedule *n.* 30
scientist *n.* 19, 23
score *v.* 69
search *v.* 10
second conditional 56
security *n.* 55
select *v.* 69
separate *adj.* 11
separate *v.* 67
sequence *n.* 35
serious *adj.* 19, 21, 67
serve *v.* 69
serving *adj.* 68
set *n.* 68
shape *v.* 59
sharp *adj.* 39
shortage *n.* 19
sickness *n.* 39
sign *v.* 32
silly *adj.* 79
since *prep.* 10
similar *adj.* 59
sing (sang, sung) *v.* 66
sit down *v.* 24
situation *n.* 70
ski *v.* 49
sky *n.* 43
slave *n.* 82
slavery *n.* 82
slow *adj.* 59
smell *v.* (smelt, smelt) 19
smoke *v.* 27
social *adj.* 23
social worker *n.* 23
society *n.* 31
solution *n.* 10
sonar *adj.* 10
sound *v.* 85
sound *v.*: Sounds great. 85
South Pole *n.* 21
Soviet *adj.* 67
So what? *idiom* 71
space *n.* 11
space plane *n.* 19
Space Shuttle *n.* 19
speaking 64
special *adj.* 10
speed *n.* 19, 66
species *n.* 39, 58
spend (*v.*) time 35
sponsor *v.* 84, 85
sport 66

sports *n.* 66
stair *n.* 63
stamp *n.* 66
statue *n.* 63
steal (stole, stolen) *v.* 71
step *n.* 59
Stonehenge *n.* 55
store *v.* 63
storey *n.* 63
straight *adv.* 79
strike *n.*: on strike 19
study *n.* 31
suggestion *n.* 35
superficial *adj.* 35
supplies *n.* 39
supporter *n.* 67
survive *v.* 59
suspend *v.* 69
suspicious *adj.* 46
swimming teacher *n.* 22

T

Taj Mahal *n.* 55
talent *n.* 22
taxi driver *n.* 22
teacher *n.* 22, 23
team *n.* 68, 70
teenage *adj.* 39
teenager *n.* 39
telephone directory *n.* 24
television *n.* 30, 31, 32, 34
telling tales 46
tepee *n.* 86
That's not on! *idiom* 71
the arts *n.* 66
threaten *v.* 85
throw (*v.*) out 61
ticket office *n.* 11
time *v.* 35
tortoise *n.* 59
total *n.* 23
touch *v.* 19, 55, 62
tournament *n.* 71
tower *n.* 63
tractor driver *n.* 23
traditional *adj.* 69
tragic *adj.* 35
trainer *n.* 71
training *n.* 66
transport *v.* 45, 50, 63
treat *v.* 82
tribal *adj.* 63
trick *v.* 71
trouble *n.* 79
trouble *n.*: to get into trouble 79
trouble *n.*: to be in trouble 47
trust *v.* 71
turn off *v.* 24
turn on *v.* 24
TV channel *n.* 19
TV news presenter *n.* 22

U

underground *adj.* 10
underneath *adv.* 63
unhappy *adj.* 31

unite *v.* 55, 62
United States of America 81
unless *conj.* 58
unusual *adj.* 58
urgent *adj.* 55
used to *v.* 11, 15
usual *adj.* 66

V

valley *n.* 61, 86
vandal *n.* 55
vandalism *n.* 55
vet *n.* 23
via *prep.*: via satellites 44
violence *n.* 67
violent *adj.* 31
virtual reality *n.* 19
visit *v.* 49
vocabulary 16
volcano *n.* 59
volleyball *n.* 68, 70

W

wall *n.* 63
war *n.* 19
was/were doing: *see past continuous* 12
was/were done: *see past passive* 68
Watch out! *interj.* 79
water *n.* 19
waterfall *n.* 87
waterproof *adj.* 51
weather forecast *n.* 43
wedding *n.* 14
weigh *v.* 59
What's up? *idiom* 71
which: *see relative clauses* 11, 15
white lie *exp.* 78
who: *see relative clauses* 11, 15
wide *adj.* 61
width *n.* 19
will 11, 14, 20
will: *see Future simple* 14
will have done: *see Future perfect* 21
wolf *n.* (*pl.* wolves) 87
wonder *v.* 79
won't *v.* 20
worked up *adj.* 71
work out *v.* 19
workshop *n.* 87
World Cup *n.* 69
World Heritage Organisation 54
world leader *n.* 21
World Wide Web *n.* 43
worry *v.*: to be worried 79
would *v.* 55
write down *v.* 24
writer *n.* 23
writing 28

Z

zero *n.* 22

Thanks and acknowledgements

Authors' thanks

The development of this course has been a large part of our lives for well over six years. During this time, we have become indebted to literally thousands of people who have so generously shared their time, skills and experience. In particular, we appreciate the constructive advice of the numerous teachers and students who helped with our initial classroom research and with the piloting, the reading and the language teaching specialists. The final version owes much to their enthusiastic involvement.

We would like to record a special 'thank you' to Peter Donovan, who shared our ideals of innovation and who has provided input and support throughout. Also to James Dingle, our editor, whose hard work, professionalism, understanding and painstaking attention to detail have helped transform our ideals into reality. We would like to express our appreciation to Maria Pylas for her careful juggling of the original manuscript. An editorial baptism by fire! It's been a great pleasure to work with her. Our thanks also to Jo Barker at CUP, our design managers, and the Gecko team for continuing their excellent work on the design of this level.

We would also like to thank the Cambridge University Press sales managers and representatives around the world for their help and support.

Finally, from Andrew, a deep appreciation of Lita, Daniel, Fiona and David tolerating a rather chaotic working life. Diana would like to dedicate this book to all those who struggle to learn and teach English and obtain books in less than comfortable conditions.

Andrew Littlejohn   Diana Hicks

The authors and publishers would like to thank the following individuals for their vital support throughout the project:

Professor Michael Breen, Edith Cowan University, Perth, Australia; Jeff Stranks, Cultura Inglesa, Rio de Janeiro, Brazil; Laura Izarra, OSEC, São Paulo, Brazil; Sergio de Souza Gabriel, Cultura Inglesa, São Paulo, Brazil; Françoise Motard, France; Eleni Miltsakaki, Athens, Greece; Akis Davanellos, The Davanellos School of Languages, Lamia, Greece; Paola Zambonelli, SMS Volta, Bologna, Italy; Cristina Zanoni, SMS Pepoli, Bologna, Italy; Emilia Paloni, SMS Lorenzo Milani, Caivano, Italy; Gisella Langé, Legnano, Italy; Mariella Merli, Milan, Italy; Roberta Fachinetti, SMS Mastri Caravaggini, Caravaggio, Italy; Giovanna Carella, SMS Nazarino Sauro, Novate Milanese, Italy; Dominique Bertrand, SMS Giacomo Leopardi, Rome, Italy; Jan Hague, British Council, Rome, Italy; Małgorzata Szwaj, English Unlimited, Gdańsk, Poland; Alistair MacLean, NKJO, Krosno, Poland; Janina Rybienik, Przemyśl, Poland; Hanna Kijowska, Warsaw, Poland; Ewa Kołodziejska, Warsaw, Poland; Zeynep Çağlar, Beyoğlu Anadolu Lisesi, Istanbul, Turkey; Maureen Günkut, Turkey.

The authors and publishers would like to thank the following institutions for their help in testing materials from this series and for the invaluable feedback which they provided:

Colegio Sion, Rio de Janeiro, Brazil; Open English House, Curitiba, Brazil; Ginásio Integrado Madalena Khan, Leblon, Brazil; Steps in English Curso Ltda., Niterói, Brazil; Instituto Educacional Stella Maris, Rio de Janeiro, Brazil; Cultura Inglesa, São Carlos, Brazil; Colegio Bandeirantes, São Paulo, Brazil; Kaumeya Language School, Alexandria, Egypt; Victory College, Victoria, Egypt; Collège Jean Jaures, Aire-sur-la-Lys, France; Collège Louis Le Prince-Ringuet, La Fare-les-Oliviers, France; Collège de Misedon, Port Brillet, France; The Aidonoupolou School, Athens, Greece; the following language school owners in Greece: Petros Dourtourekas, Athens; Eleni Fakalou, Athens; Angeliki & Lance Kinnick, Athens; Mark Palmer, Athens; Georgia Stamatopoulou, Athens; Anna Zerbini-Vasiliadou, Athens; Shirley Papanikolaou, Heraklion; Tony Hatzinikolaou, Kos; Antonis Trechas, Piraeus; SMS Italo Calvino, Milan, Italy; SMS G Rodari, Novate Milanese, Italy; SMS L Fibonacci, Pisa, Italy; Accademia Britannica/International House, Rome, Italy; David English House, Hiroshima, Japan; British Council, Tokyo, Japan; Senri International School, Japan; Szkol/a Podstawowa w Bratkówce, Poland; Primary School, Debowiec, Poland; English Unlimited, Gdańsk, Poland; 4th Independent Primary School, Kraków, Poland; Gama Bell School School of English, Kraków, Poland; Kosmopolita, Łódź, Poland; Private Language School PRIME, Łódź, Poland; Szkoła Społeczna 2001, Łódź, Poland; Szkoła Podstawowa Nr 11, Nowy Sacz, Poland; Omnibus, Poznań, Poland; Szkoła Języków Obcych J. Rybienik i A. Ochalskiej, Przemyśl, Poland; Szkoła Podstawowa Nr 23, Warsaw, Poland; Szkoła Podstawowa Nr 320, Warsaw, Poland; Liceum Ogólnokształcące Wschowa, Poland; Yukselis Koleji I, Ankara, Turkey; Özel Kalamis Lisesi, Istanbul, Turkey; Özel Sener Lisesi, Istanbul, Turkey.

The authors and publishers would like to thank the following for all their help in the production of the finished materials:

Gecko Limited, Bicester, Oxon for all stages of design and production: particular thanks to David Evans, James Arnold, Wendy Homer, Linda Beveridge and Sharon Ryan; Goodfellow & Egan, Cambridge for colour scanning and reproduction. Particular thanks to David Ward; Sandie Huskinson-Rolfe of photoseekers for picture research; Nigel Luckhurst & Jules Selmes for photographs; Brian Martin and students at the City of Ely Community College; Nick Williams and students at Netherhall Upper School, Cambridge; Heather Richards for help with selecting artists; Janet and Peter Simmonett for freelance design work; Martin Williamson (Prolingua Productions), Diana and Peter Thompson (Studio AVP) and all of the actors who contributed to the recordings.

The authors and publishers are grateful to the following illustrators and photographic sources:

Illustrators: Gerry Ball: pp. 12 *br*, 14 *m* 74; Kathy Baxendale: handwriting; Felicity Roma Bowers: textured backgrounds; Rob Calow: p. 42; Goodfellow & Egan: DTP maps; Phil Healey: pp. 16, 28, 52, 64: Steve Lach: p. 45 *l*; Sarah McMenemy: pp. 25 *r*, 57 and exercise icons; David Mitcheson: pp. 14 *t* & *b*, 37; Michael Ogden: p. 24; Alan Peacock: handwriting; John Plumb: p. 34; Chris Riley: p. 87; Martin Sanders: pp. 11 *t*,18, 19, 20, 61; James Sneddon: pp. 8, 9, 12, 66, 70, 74, 77, 92; John Storey p. 73; Stuart Williams: pp. 32, 33;

Photographic sources: Action-Plus/Glyn Kirk: p. 31 *b*; Francois Gohier/Ardea London: pp. 61 *m*, 86 (6), Liz and Tony Bomford/Ardea London: p. 15 *b*; Tom Willock/Ardea: p. 86 (2); Art Directors/Trip/M. Lee: p 55 *t*; Axiom Photographic Agency/Jim Holmes: p. 23 *t* (5); Anthony Blake Photo Library: pp. 23 *t* (3); Britstock/West Stock/Anderson: p. 82 *bl*; Camera Press London/Erma: p. 10; Canadian Tourism Commission; pp. 86 (1) & (5), 87 *l*; The J. Allan Cash Photolibrary: pp. 55 *m*, 61 *t*, 81 *br*; Sylvain Grandadam/Colorific; p 58 *tr*, Comstock Inc.: p. 23 *t* (2); Empics/Sven Simon: p.69 *t*; Mary Evans Picture Library: p. 11 *m*; Eye Ubiquitous/S. Greenland: p. 13 *b*; Eye Ubiquitous/J.B Pickering: p. 84 *b*; Michael Ann Mullen/Format: p. 23 *bl*; Melanie Friend/Format: p. 84 *tr*, Getty Images: p. 10 *t*; Getty Images/Steven Weinberg; Scott Barrow/International Stock/Robert Harding Picture Library: p. 31 *br*; Duncan Maxwell/RHPL: p. 13 *t*; Robert Harding Picture Library/Walter Rawlings: p. 63 *tr*; RHPL/Roy Rainford: p. 86 (3); Robert Francis/Hutchinson: p. 84 *tl*; The Image Bank/L. D. Gordon: p. 15 *r*, /Wendy Chan; Images Colour Library: pp. 23 *br*, 59, 63 *b*, 81 *tl* & *bm*, 90 *b*; Ben Edwards/Impact Photos: p. 11 *ml*; Alain Le Garsmeur/Impact: p. 66 *tr*; Columbia (courtesy Kobal): p. 60 *m*; Lucasfilm/20th Century Fox (courtesy Kobal): p. 18 *br*; Frank Lane Picture Library/Foto Natura: p. 23 *r*; Paul Velasco/Link: p. 67 *t*; Nigel Luckhurst: pp. 27, 30, 31 (TV screens), 35, 36, 44, 46, 47, 71, 78, 79, 85; Nahanni National Park Reserve, USA: p. 87 *r*; Peter Newark's Pictures: p. 82 & *m*; Brian Hawkes/NHPA: p. 60 *t*; Marc Schlossman/Panos Pictures: p. 66 *mr*; Jim Holmes/Panos: p. 66 *bl*; courtesy Paramount Pictures Corporation: p. 18 *bl*; Pictor International: pp. 23 *t* (1), 42, 60 *b*, 66 *ml*, 81 *ml*, 88; Popperfoto/UPI: pp. 15 *l*, 39 *tl* & *b*; c Oxfam United Kingdom and Ireland: p. 60 *m*; Redferns/Pete Cronin: p. 31 (C); Rex Features Limited/Simisa: p. 67 *b*; Spectrum Colour Library: pp. 55 *bl* & *br*, 63 *tl*; The Stock Market: pp. 23 *t* (4), 24, 31 (A), 66 *br*, 112 *l*; Tony Stone Images/Paul Damien: p. 81 *cr*; Archives Humanité/ Bernard Annebicque/Sygma: p. 22 *l*; Topham Picturepoint: p. 12 *tr*, Toyota (GB) Limited: p. 31 (D); TSI/Peter Correz: p. 81 *tr*, TSI/Art Wolfe: pp. 62, 86 (4), TSI/Hideo Kurihara: p. 58 *bl*, TSI/Ian Murphy: p. 58 *r*, TSI/James Martin: p. 59 *t*, TSI/Michael Scott: p. 61 *b*, TSI/Robert Frerck: pp. 86-87 background, TSI/William S. Helsel: p. 88 *t*, TSI/D.E. Cox: p. 89 *t*; Superstock Limited: p. 82 *t*; Pascal Tournaire/Sygma: p. 39 *tr*, John Walmsley: p. 23 *bm*; Zefa Pictures: pp. 82 *cl*, 43.

t = top *m* = middle *b* = bottom *r* = right *c* = centre *l* = left *u* = upper *low* = lower

Picture research by Sandie Huskinson-Rolfe of photoseekers.

Cover illustration by Felicity Roma Bowers.
Cover design by Dunne & Scully.
Design and production handled by Gecko Limited, Bicester, Oxon.
Sound recordings by Martin Williamson, Prolingua Productions, at Studio AVP.
American sound recordings by Rich Le Page.